M000251183

GOD HAS LEFT THE BUILDING

DAVID M. REVELL

ISBN 978-1-63844-320-9 (paperback)
ISBN 978-1-63844-321-6 (digital)

Copyright © 2021 by David M. Revell

All rights reserved. No part of this publication may be reproduced, distributed, or transmitted in any form or by any means, including photocopying, recording, or other electronic or mechanical methods without the prior written permission of the publisher. For permission requests, solicit the publisher via the address below.

Christian Faith Publishing, Inc.
832 Park Avenue
Meadville, PA 16335
www.christianfaithpublishing.com

Printed in the United States of America

To my precious wife, and all God's gift to us in our family; children, grandchildren, great grandchildren, and all our extended family; to our wonderful church family, brothers and sisters in Christ; and to Mom—an astute Bible student and teacher.

So then faith cometh by hearing, and hearing by the
word of God. But I say, Have they not heard?
Yes verily, their sound went into all the earth,
and their words unto the ends of the world.

—Romans 10:17–18 KJV

CONTENTS

Foreword

> Man shall not live by bread alone, but by every word that proceedeth out of the mouth of God.
>
> —Matthew 4:3–4 KJV

This brief foreword is to provide a stepping stone into some of the lessons you might have missed in Sunday school or just skipped over in your daily reading of the historical narratives. I personally have not heard these lessons as messages or sermons in church, ever—though I confess I may not always have been listening as carefully as I should.

Perhaps we do not take seriously enough the words of Jesus as quoted above. In my first real pastorate, I startled myself during one Sunday morning sermon by realizing in the middle of it that I would not walk across the street to hear me preach. What a revelation! In my second pastorate, I found myself weeping over personal inadequacies, presumed failures of character, and an unreasonable fear that some demonic influence kept me from a successful preaching and thus a successful ministry.

God spoke to me clearly one morning in the midst of beating myself up over all this. His answer to me was simply, and I quote, "Son, put up your books and tapes and get into my Word." There immediately came a hunger for the very Word of God, not just commentaries and the tape ministries so prolific in the 1970s. That revelation led to graduate school with a degree in biblical studies and an expanded zeal for expository preaching and teaching.

> And further, by these, my son, be admonished: of making many books there is no end; and much study is a weariness of the flesh. (Ecclesiastes 12:12 KJV)

So, at the urging of people that I dearly love and appreciate, I am adding one more book. With it comes an important disclaimer.

I have not always been careful with referencing my sources. I regret this omission, but in my defense, these messages were designed to be preached with the barest of outlines, the reading of the scripture, and the giving of the sense of it with the occasional illustration or personal story. I have learned so much from those I consider giants in biblical study, in theology, in preaching the Word. There was a college assignment of one hundred hours reading on Isaiah, a multiplicity of sermons both in person and readings, and perhaps hundreds of books that I lugged around in the early years of ministry and finally gave away to Christian schools. Who could count what I learned and preached but failed to refer to strict AMA, ADA, ASA, ACS, ACM, and Turabian codes?

So here are some messages that I have preached and taught over the years from the biblical narrative. I present them in the hope that you will find them interesting, enlightening, and encouraging to *hearing the Word of God* in its fullness.

Preface

The word "pulpit" is found only once in the King James Version of the Bible. It referred to a wooden structure upon which Ezra, the scribe, stood to read the Word of God to those who returned from the captivity. Ezra and the other readers mentioned by name, "read in the book in the law of God distinctly, and gave the sense, and caused them to understand the reading" (Nehemiah 8:8 KJV).

Each of the following messages was designed for that exact purpose: that is to be preached and understood. They may seem to lose some force in the transition to "plain text," but it could be that you will still hear the thunder in the voices of the prophets and apostles.

The Restoration of the Leper

When he was come down from the mountain, great multitudes followed him. And, behold, there came a leper and worshipped him, saying, Lord, if thou wilt, thou canst make me clean. And Jesus put forth his hand, and touched him, saying, I will; be thou clean. And immediately his leprosy was cleansed. And Jesus saith unto him, See thou tell no man; but go thy way, shew thyself to the priest, and offer the gift that Moses commanded, for a testimony unto them.

—Matthew 8:1–4 KJV

Just across the bay from the great fortress El Morrow in San Juan, Puerto Rico is a small island named Isla de Cabras, or Goat Island. There is a smaller fort there, Fortin San Juan de la Cruz, designed to provide a crossfire as part of the defenses of San Juan Harbor. In the late 1800s, the island was designated as a leper colony and the 1910 census listed only thirty-five inhabitants. It was a stark reminder of a fearful disease that has ravaged individuals and families from the earliest days of recorded history.

Leprosy, or Hansen's disease, is a chronic infectious disease that affects the skin and peripheral nerves, sometimes affecting the nose and eyes as well. It is characterized by scabs, various sores, and white spots on and beneath the skin. The root word in Hebrew has to do with scales, peeling, or flaking. However, the word translated leper or leprous could mean any number of different skin diseases, including leprosy.

Though not considered highly contagious today, throughout the Old Testament leprosy was considered a death sentence, even a judgment from God. For example, in the account of Aaron and Miriam speaking against their brother Moses because of his Ethiopian wife, God called all three of them out to the tabernacle. Moses, named here the meekest man on the whole earth, apparently had no clue what was going on. Aaron and Miriam, though, were rebuked for their rebellious and seditious speech. The cloud of God's glory, his manifest presence, lifted, and…

> Behold, Miriam became leprous, white as snow: and Aaron looked upon Miriam, and, behold, she was leprous. And Aaron said unto Moses, Alas, my lord, I beseech thee, lay not the sin upon us, wherein we have done foolishly, and wherein we have sinned. Let her not be as one dead. (Numbers 12:10–12 KJV)

With this background in mind, the leprous man braving the multitudes to appear before Jesus was taking his life in his hands. His faith was such that he believed that Jesus could cleanse him of the dread disease. There is no hint of how far along the disease had taken this man, but in Christ alone was hope that he could indeed be free of the curse if the Lord was willing. Jesus's answer should give hope to all who seek him.

> And Jesus put forth his hand, and touched him, saying, I will; be thou clean. (Matthew 8:3 KJV)

Immediately, the Scriptures record that his leprosy was cleansed. Perhaps as amazing, Jesus had reached out and touched him. It is quite likely that he had not been touched by anyone in a long time.

Then Jesus, the Jewish Messiah, gave what we might call *follow-up* instructions. It is important to remember that Jesus, the very Son of God, was "born of a woman, born under the law, to redeem them that were under the law" (Galatians 4:4). The instructions were in accordance with the law of Moses and the prescribed sacrifices for those who had been healed or cleansed from leprosy.

> And Jesus saith unto him, See thou tell no man; but go thy way, shew thyself to the priest, and offer the gift that Moses commanded, for a testimony unto them. (Matthew 8:4 KJV)

There was an offering commanded (offer the gift) in the law (that Moses commanded) upon the cleansing of a leper. From the apostle Paul, we see its application to us on this side of the cross:

> Now all these things happened unto them for ensamples: and they are written for our admonition, upon whom the ends of the world are come. (1 Corinthians 10:11 KJV)

As Matthew Henry observes in this passage: "every disease is both the fruit of sin, and a figure of it, as the disorder of the soul" (MHC). All of the Old Testament sacrifices point to the Redeemer, the Messiah, who would bring both healing and cleansing to a sin-sick world.

There were four steps in this whole process and each step was outlined in Leviticus, the priest's handbook, chapters 13–14.

Step One: Contamination

> And the Lord spake unto Moses and Aaron, saying, When a man shall have in the skin of his flesh a rising, a scab, or a bright spot, and it be in the skin of his flesh like the plague of leprosy. (Leviticus 13:1–3)

"Germs and Jesus!" exclaimed the little boy to his grandmother. "That's all I hear, and I have never seen either one!"

When God brought out the children of Abraham from four hundred years of slavery, he revealed himself to them in manifest appearance by the cloud and the fire on their journey. As this vast congregation gathered at Mt. Sinai, they saw the God of heaven and earth descend and speak to them. Beyond these manifestations to that particular generation, God gave the Law. That Law was a further revelation of God's character and attributes. Included in that law were some very specific rules for diet and hygiene.

> And said, If thou wilt diligently hearken to the voice of the Lord thy God, and wilt do that which is right in his sight, and wilt give ear to his commandments, and keep all his statutes, I will put none of these diseases upon thee, which I have brought upon the Egyptians: for I am the Lord that healeth thee. (Exodus 15:26 KJV)

Though the children of Israel did not have the modern understanding of germs and microorganisms, much less the technology to deal with them, if they obeyed the Law of God they would walk in general health and blessing. As a person may not understand where or how they got leprosy, it is the same with sin.

> Behold, I was shapen in iniquity; and in sin did my mother conceive me. (Psalm 51:5 KJV)

> For all have sinned, and come short of the glory of God. (Romans 3:23 KJV)

As Woody declared in the cartoon movie *Toy Story*, "Somebody's poisoned the waterhole!" The theological doctrine of original sin is played out before us every day. The three-year-old that shakes his fist at his mother and shouts a defiant "No!" is an illustration of that fact. He did not get that rebellious nature from public school or playing with the deacon's kids or poor potty training. It is an ingrained nature that if not corrected will result in his utter destruction.

Step Two: Examination

> Then he shall be brought unto Aaron the priest, or unto one of his sons the priests: And the priest shall look on the plague in the skin of the flesh: and when the hair in the plague is turned white, and the plague in sight be deeper than the skin of his flesh, it is a plague of leprosy: and the priest shall look on him, and pronounce him unclean. (Leviticus 13:1–3)

> The priest is to go outside the camp and examine him. (Leviticus 14:3 NIV)

God had provided detailed information to the priesthood regarding leprosy and other skin diseases. Leprosy was distinguished from balding, boils, and other natural but non-lethal problems with an examination by the priest. The nature of a man would be to look at the plague in his flesh and dismiss it, much like people today rationalize their sin nature.

> Every way of a man is right in his own eyes, But the LORD weighs the hearts. (Proverbs 21:2 NKJV)

Paul reminds us that even our judgment of ourselves may be inaccurate and biased.

> But with me it is a very small thing that I should be judged by you or by a human court. In fact, I do not even judge myself. For I know of nothing against myself, yet I am not justified by this; but He who judges me is the Lord. Therefore judge nothing before the time, until the Lord comes, who will both bring to light the hidden things of darkness and reveal the counsels of the hearts. Then each one's praise will come from God. (1 Corinthians 4:3–5 NKJV)

There is One that judges accurately and fairly in absolute perfection.

> For the word of God is living and powerful, and sharper than any two-edged sword, piercing even to the division of soul and spirit, and of joints and marrow, and is a Discerner of the thoughts and intents of the heart. And there is no creature hidden from His sight, but all things are naked and open to the eyes of Him to whom we must give account. (Hebrews 4:11–13 KJV)

Our own judgments and the judgments of others pale in significance to the perfect judgment of the omniscient, omnipotent, and omnipresent God of heaven and earth.

Step Three: Separation

> But if the priest look on it, and, behold, there be no white hair in the bright spot, and it be no lower than the other skin, but be somewhat dark; then the priest shall shut him up seven days: And the priest shall look upon him the seventh day: and if it be spread much abroad in the skin, then the priest shall pronounce him unclean: it is the plague of leprosy. (Leviticus 13:26–27 KJV)

Here in the Old Testament is the early model of quarantine. Because the diagnosis was unclear, the priest would separate the person for seven days. There was even an option for another seven days provided in the Law if the diagnosis was still unclear. Our modern word *quarantine* comes from the Italian *quarantina*. It referred to a required separation of forty days imposed upon ships coming into the harbor from other countries that could bring deadly and contagious diseases in the early 1600s. Quarantine is a biblical concept.

It is sin that has separated us from God. The Scriptures speak clearly to the issue and definition of sin and death.

> And the Lord God formed man of the dust of the ground, and breathed into his nostrils the breath of life; and man became a living soul. (Genesis 2:7 KJV)

Death is the obvious separation of life from the body, just as sin separated mankind from a holy God. The body lies inanimate in death because the life has gone. The apostle Paul expounds upon this separation.

> Wherefore, as by one man sin entered into the world, and death by sin; and so death passed upon all men, for that all have sinned. (Romans 5:12 KJV)

> Once you were alienated from God and were enemies in your minds because of your evil behavior. (Colossians 1:21–23)

This reality is expressed consistently all over the world. In examples as plain as a child set in the corner for misbehaving to the execution of murderers by a just society, sin causes separation. Sin breaks up families, puts people in jail, and divides nations. The ultimate separation is separation from God. Though we are separated from God by our sin now, the final separation by judgment is called the second death (Revelation 20:14).

Step Four: Restoration

> And the Lord spake unto Moses, saying, This shall be the law of the leper in the day of his cleansing: He shall be brought unto the priest: And the priest shall go forth out of the camp; and the priest shall look, and, behold, if the plague of leprosy be healed in the leper; Then shall the priest command to take for him that is to be cleansed two birds alive and clean, and cedar wood, and scarlet, and hyssop: And the priest shall command that one of the birds be killed in an earthen vessel over running water: As for the living bird, he shall take it, and the cedar wood, and the scarlet, and the hyssop, and shall dip them

> and the living bird in the blood of the bird that was killed over the running water: And he shall sprinkle upon him that is to be cleansed from the leprosy seven times, and shall pronounce him clean, and shall let the living bird loose into the open field. (Leviticus 14:1–7 KJV)

There is good news in all this. This is the description very gift Jesus required of the man healed of leprosy as he showed his healing to the priests. If the priests could see that the person is truly healed and cleansed from the dread disease, then the offering was made for restoration.

It is here in this Old Testament picture that we see clearly what restoration means and how it is accomplished. Of the two sacrificial birds, one was chosen for death and its blood poured out. The second, still living, was dipped into the blood of the first. This blood was sprinkled seven times, indicating completeness, upon the person declared clean of leprosy. The living bird was then set free into the open field.

How clearly this speaks to us of the One who became like us, our Immanuel—God with us!

> And the Word was made flesh, and dwelt among us, (and we beheld his glory, the glory as of the only begotten of the Father,) full of grace and truth. (John 1:14 KJV)

> Wherefore in all things it behoved him to be made like unto his brethren, that he might be a merciful and faithful high priest in things pertaining to God, to make reconciliation for the sins of the people. (Hebrews 2:17 KJV)

The very Word of God become flesh and willingly died for the sins of the world (John 3:16). As the Scripture declares, he was "made of a woman, made under the law, to redeem them that were under the law" (Galatians 4:4). He was the same as his brethren. He was human.

Following the sequence, like as the second bird was dipped into the blood of the first, so we are saved by the blood of our Lord Jesus Christ.

> How much more shall the blood of Christ, who through the eternal Spirit offered himself without spot to God, purge your conscience from dead works to serve the living God? And for this cause he is the mediator of the new testament, that by means of death, for the redemption of the transgressions that were under the first testament, they which are called might receive the promise of eternal inheritance. (Hebrews 9:14–15 KJV)

Here as well we see that the second bird once dipped into the blood of the first, was taken to an open field and released, and set free. Redeemed by the precious blood of Jesus, we too are set free.

> For as by one man's disobedience many were made sinners, so by the obedience of one shall many be made righteous. Moreover the law entered, that the offence might abound. But where sin abounded, grace did much more abound: That as sin hath reigned unto death, even so might grace reign through righteousness unto eternal life by Jesus Christ our Lord. (Romans 5:19–21 KJV)

It might be said that the most dangerous gift God has given to man is the gift of freedom. How then shall we live?

> For whether we live, we live unto the Lord; and whether we die, we die unto the Lord: whether we live therefore, or die, we are the Lord's. (Romans 14:8 KJV)

Prayer

Father, you have set us free through the precious blood of the Lord Jesus Christ. Forgive us when we unthinkingly turn back to bondage whether in thought or deed. Help us to walk in the Spirit of liberty with joyfulness and thankfulness. Amen.

The Captivity

By the rivers of Babylon, there we sat down, yea, we wept, when we remembered Zion. We hanged our harps upon the willows in the midst thereof. For there they that carried us away captive required of us a song; and they that wasted us required of us mirth, saying, Sing us one of the songs of Zion. How shall we sing the Lord's song in a strange land? If I forget thee, O Jerusalem, let my right hand forget her cunning. If I do not remember thee, let my tongue cleave to the roof of my mouth; if I prefer not Jerusalem above my chief joy. Remember, O Lord, the children of Edom in the day of Jerusalem; who said, Rase it, rase it, even to the foundation thereof. O daughter of Babylon, who art to be destroyed; happy shall he be, that rewardeth thee as thou hast served us. Happy shall he be, that taketh and dasheth thy little ones against the stones.

—Psalm 137 KJV

The year 605 BC was a horror for the people and the land of Israel. It was a nightmare from which they would not awaken. The worst was still to come.

It began with the death of their beloved King Josiah. Jeremiah the prophet began his ministry as a young man of about twenty in the thirteenth year of King Josiah's reign, about 627 BC. Israel was a land in the middle of what we now call the Middle East. Being in the middle is a dangerous place. In 609 BC, the armies of Egypt under Pharaoh Necho moved northward through Israel to stop the advance of a burgeoning Babylon. Warned not to interfere, King Josiah advanced nevertheless against the Egyptian might and was killed in battle (2 Chronicles 35). Later, in the decisive battle of Carchemish, 605 BC, Nebuchadnezzar proved himself an able general and proved Babylon a world power by defeating Egypt. A defeated Egypt retreated back through Israel, deposing the new king, Jehoahaz, after a brief three-month reign and deporting him to Egypt where he died.

He was replaced by Jehoiakim who himself had to face Nebuchadnezzar again just a few years later. Forced under tribute, Jehoiakim gave up the treasures of the temple and the very finest of the people, including some of the royal family and Daniel, Hananiah, Mishael, and Azariah (Daniel 1). (The latter three may be better known by their Babylonian names Shadrach, Meshach, and Abednego.)

Nebuchadnezzar returned to the throne of Babylon at the death of his father, Nabopolassar, and apparently needed a strong infrastructure and administrative base.

From the book of Daniel, we understand these Hebrew captives soon rose to power and influence in Babylon.

The reign of Jehoiakim, however, continued an unmitigated disaster. His rebellious nature brought the wrath of Nebuchadnezzar against him again, and in 597 BC, he was unceremoniously deposed. Josephus records that Nebuchadnezzar had Jehoiakim's body thrown from the city wall, unburied. It may have been here as well that the temple was looted. At this point, Nebuchadnezzar took 10,000 captives from Israel, including some of the nobility, Ezekiel, and skilled craftsmen like carpenters and smiths. Unlike the Assyrian conquerors before them, the Babylonians understood that dead people do not pay tribute, nor do they contribute to empire building. These captives were transported to Babylon and forced to settle in by the River Chebar (though it was more likely not a river at all but one of Babylon's famed canals).

Only the prophet Jeremiah and the poorest of the people remained in Israel. In this troubled time, it is interesting to note that God had specific, chosen men for prophetic ministry in precisely those places where they were most needed—Daniel in Babylon proper, Ezekiel with the captive community at Chebar, and Jeremiah with the remaining Israelites in Jerusalem.

It was here at Chebar that Ezekiel received his first vision and prophetic call. It was here as well that Jeremiah's letter to the captives was read (Jeremiah 29).

> Now these are the words of the letter that
> Jeremiah the prophet sent from Jerusalem

> unto the residue of the elders which were carried away captives, and to the priests, and to the prophets, and to all the people whom Nebuchadnezzar had carried away captive from Jerusalem to Babylon. (Jeremiah 29:1)

> Thus saith the Lord of hosts, the God of Israel, unto all that are carried away captives, whom I have caused to be carried away from Jerusalem unto Babylon; Build ye houses, and dwell in them; and plant gardens, and eat the fruit of them; Take ye wives, and beget sons and daughters; and take wives for your sons, and give your daughters to husbands, that they may bear sons and daughters; that ye may be increased there, and not diminished. And seek the peace of the city whither I have caused you to be carried away captives, and pray unto the Lord for it: for in the peace thereof shall ye have peace. (Jeremiah 29:4–7 KJV)

And it was here at Chebar that God's people refused to play their native songs in the strange land of Babylon with its strange speech and strange customs. It was here that they wept together at the memory of their homeland, hanging their musical instruments on the trees.

> For there they that carried us away captive required of us a song; and they that wasted us required of us mirth, saying, Sing us one of the songs of Zion. How shall we sing the Lord's song in a strange land? (Psalm 137:3–4 KJV)

While various prophets were preaching the destruction of Babylon and the return of the captives within a few years, it had been revealed to Jeremiah that their captivity would last seventy years. There was the promise of the return of the exiles, but a time for their return was set in the future.

> For thus saith the Lord of hosts, the God of Israel; Let not your prophets and your diviners, that be in the midst of you, deceive you, neither hearken to your dreams which ye cause to be dreamed. For they prophesy falsely unto you in my name: I have not sent them, saith the Lord. For thus saith the Lord, That after seventy years be accomplished at Babylon I will visit you, and perform my good word toward you, in causing you to return to this place. (Jeremiah 29:8–10 KJV)

It was this very prophecy that came into the hands of Daniel that caused him to understand that the seventy years were nearly fulfilled.

> In the first year of his reign I Daniel understood by books the number of the years, whereof the word of the Lord came to Jeremiah the prophet, that he would accomplish seventy years in the desolations of Jerusalem. (Daniel 9:2 KJV)

Not only would the people of the captivity not sing their Jewish songs and not play their instruments, but also they brought themselves under a curse if they lost memory of Jerusalem and home.

> If I forget thee, O Jerusalem, let my right hand forget her cunning. If I do not remember thee, let my tongue cleave to the roof of my mouth; if I prefer not Jerusalem above my chief joy. (Psalm 137:5–6 KJV)

After seventy years, the force of the curse had lessened considerably. When Ezra and Nehemiah assembled people under King Cyrus to return, they found that most people had become used to their new land and were doing quite well there. Only a fraction of the exiles returned to rebuild.

A second curse was placed upon the Edomites who were complicit in the destruction of Jerusalem. Their battle cry was to completely erase the city, to raze it to the ground. There had been bad blood between Israel and Edom for generations, and the Edomites rejoiced to see the destruction of Jerusalem, even to the point of giving helpful directions to the Babylonians during the siege.

However, the brunt of their animus was reserved for Babylon itself. This Psalm, and Psalms like it that call for vengeance and retribution, are often called imprecatory Psalms. When the great psalmist David called for God to *break the teeth* of the wicked, he was calling for justice to be rendered. No doubt, the call for the destruction of Babylon had this element, but their vindictive anger went even further.

> Happy shall he be, that taketh and dasheth thy little ones against the stones. (Psalm 137:9 KJV)

Because such a sentence is in the Bible, it could be easy to forget that the Old Testament often called for justice in the form of *an eye for an eye.* Unless you have seen firsthand the destruction and misery brought on by war, you may have trouble empathizing with the exiles. Collateral damage is not just a modern issue, but a fact of life confirmed throughout the Scriptures and all of history. The chilling expression of anger and hatred displayed in this Psalm was not, and is not, unique.

To understand this disturbing bit of history through God's eyes requires the hermeneutic principle of allowing the Scriptures to interpret Scriptures. To discover that viewpoint we need to look at a vision of Jeremiah, the prophet remaining in the ravaged and burned out land of Israel. Here is the vision of Jeremiah:

> The Lord shewed me, and, behold, two baskets of figs were set before the temple of the Lord, after that Nebuchadrezzar king of Babylon had carried away captive Jeconiah the son of Jehoiakim king of Judah, and the princes of Judah, with the carpenters and smiths, from Jerusalem, and had brought them to Babylon. One basket had very good figs, even like the figs that are first ripe: and the other basket had very naughty figs, which could not be eaten, they were so bad. Then said the Lord unto me, What seest thou, Jeremiah? And I said, Figs; the good figs, very good; and the evil, very evil, that cannot be eaten, they are so evil. (Jeremiah 24:1–3 KJV)

This vision of the two baskets of figs was given to Jeremiah following the second invasion by Nebuchadnezzar. Jeconiah, also called Jehoichin, reigned in Jerusalem three months after the death of Jehoiakim and surrendered the city to Nebuchadnezzar and was exiled with others of the royal family. There remained only one last Babylon invasion in 586 BC that completely destroyed Jerusalem and its temple. It is recorded that Nebuchadnezzar's captain of the guard, Nebuzaradan, "left certain of the poor of the land for vinedressers and for husbandmen" (Jeremiah 52:16 KJV) while almost everyone else was killed or carried away into Babylon.

The Lord himself explains to Jeremiah the meaning of the two baskets of figs.

> Thus saith the Lord, the God of Israel; Like these good figs, so will I acknowledge them that are carried away captive of Judah, whom I have sent out of this place into the land of the Chaldeans for their good. For I will set mine eyes upon them for good, and I will bring them again to this land: and I will build them, and not pull them down; and I will plant them, and not pluck them up. And I will give them an heart to know me, that I am the Lord: and they shall be my people, and I will be their God: for they shall return unto me with their whole heart. (Jeremiah 24:5–7 KJV)

From God's plan and purpose, those carried away captive to Babylon, those angry exiles who refused to sing the Lord's song in a strange land, those bitter captives who longed for the destruction of Babylonian babies—they were the good figs! God's promise to them was that he had taken them out for their own good and that he would bring them back with a heart to know him and acknowledge him. In their shortsightedness, in their anger, and in their frustration, they had missed the promise of God for their restoration. They had lost sight of the very nature of God, his love, his purpose. Listen to the last part of the letter from Jeremiah, which says:

> For I know the thoughts that I think toward you, saith the Lord, thoughts of peace, and not of evil, to give you an expected end. Then shall ye call upon me, and ye shall go and pray unto me, and I will hearken unto you. And ye shall seek me, and find me, when ye shall search for me with all your heart. And I will be found of you, saith the Lord: and I will turn away your captivity, and I will gather you from all the nations, and from all the places whither I have driven you, saith the Lord; and I will bring you again into the place whence I caused you to be carried away captive. (Jeremiah 29:11–14 KJV)

How quickly we as well forget where we are in God's grand design as we navigate the trials and disappointments of our lives. How quickly we turn away from the promise of God from the apostle Paul:

> For I consider that the sufferings of this present time are not worthy to be compared with the glory that is to be revealed to us. For the anxious longing of the creation waits eagerly for the revealing of the sons of God. For the creation was sub-

> jected to futility, not willingly, but because of Him who subjected it, in hope that the creation itself also will be set free from its slavery to corruption into the freedom of the glory of the children of God. And we know that God causes all things to work together for good to those who love God, to those who are called according to His purpose. (Romans 8:15–32)

Prayer

Gracious Father, you have promised your children that you will make all things new and that all things work together for good to them that love you. You also know that we are dust. We see through a glass darkly. Forgive us that we cannot always see your precious hand in the things that affect our lives. Help us to discern clearly the working of the Spirit in bringing us to maturity.

Forbidden Areas of Division

> And the Lord God said, It is not good that the man should be alone; I will make him an help meet for him.
>
> —Genesis 2:18 KJV

After a wonderful series of creation events that God said were good, he comes to the last day of creation and declares that it was all very good.

> And God saw every thing that he had made, and, behold, it was very good. And the evening and the morning were the sixth day. (Genesis 1:31 KJV)

There was only one thing in all his creation that God found not good. Of all the creatures God had made, Adam was the only one created in the image of God. He did not have a *helpmeet,* a suitable counterpart.

Why did God see a *not good*? A popular song back in the day sang mournfully that *one is the loneliest number*. It has been said that one is aloneness, two is relationship and intimacy, and three is communion and fellowship. Before creation, there had actually never been *aloneness* before. It is plain that God made man (mankind), "male and female made He them" (Genesis 1:27). Though some have intimated that woman was an afterthought with God, nothing could be further from the truth. In God's creation of living things, he included reproduction, each kind with male and female, even in the plants. The command to *be fruitful, and multiply* was given to all living things (Genesis 1:22).

After mankind fell away from God and sin entered the picture, the relationships were damaged: man to God, man to woman, man to man, man to creation. Left alone in spiritual death, it did not take long for all the works of the flesh to manifest (Galatians 5).

> And God saw that the wickedness of man was great in the earth, and that every imagination of the thoughts of his heart was only evil continually. (Genesis 6:5 KJV)

> The earth also was corrupt before God, and the earth was filled with violence. And God looked upon the earth, and, behold, it was corrupt; for all flesh had corrupted his way upon the earth. (Genesis 6:11–12 KJV)

In righteous judgment, there was a flood over all the earth but "Noah found grace in the eyes of the Lord" (Genesis 6:8). Beyond much of the early history, God came to a place in his gracious plan to restore mankind where he revealed himself again to Moses and the children of Israel in the giving of the Ten Commandments. This was a fresh revealing of his nature and a call to return to that image, to once again reflect the nature of God.

For instance, why the prohibition against bearing false witness, lying? We look to the nature of God:

> God is not a man, that he should lie; neither the son of man, that he should repent: hath he said, and shall he not do it? or hath he spoken, and shall he not make it good? (Numbers 23:19 KJV)

> Every good gift and every perfect gift is from above, and cometh down from the Father of lights, with whom is no variableness, neither shadow of turning. Of his own will begat he us with the word of truth. (James 1:17–18 KJV)

In another instance, why would God say (Malachi 2), "I hate divorce?" Because it is contrary to his nature. It is destructive rather than building up, harmful rather than helpful. There is no division in God (John 1:1).

> I and My Father are one. (John 10:30 KJV)

The nature of God is reflected in his creation and the social order he created, the social institutions of family and church. So, we have Christ who honors the Father, the wife who honors the husband, and the commandment to the children to honor father and mother. Unwilling to accept the ideas of authority and submission, many in the world hate this idea of the natural roles. In what is called his high priestly prayer, Jesus sought unity for his people, with no division.

> I pray for them: I pray not for the world, but for them which thou hast given me; for they are thine. And all mine are thine, and thine are mine; and I am glorified in them. And now I am no more in the world, but these are in the world, and I come to thee. Holy Father, keep through thine own name those whom thou hast given me, that they may be one, as we are. (John 17:9–11 KJV)

If we are indeed to reflect this unity, this Oneness, the people of God must take this seriously. There are areas of our lives where the Scriptures plainly forbid division within the church. We are not to separate ourselves from others in the faith.

1. Spiritual leaders, instruments of salvation

> Now I beseech you, brethren, by the name of our Lord Jesus Christ, that ye all speak the same thing, and that there be no divi-

> sions among you; but that ye be perfectly joined together in the same mind and in the same judgment. For it hath been declared unto me of you, my brethren, by them which are of the house of Chloe, that there are contentions among you. Now this I say, that every one of you saith, I am of Paul; and I of Apollos; and I of Cephas; and I of Christ. Is Christ divided? was Paul crucified for you? or were ye baptized in the name of Paul? (1 Corinthians 1:10–13 KJV)

Though it is apparently a common practice in the church at large, the naming of denominations or movements after leaders seems to have been forbidden to the early church. The apostle Paul declares it to be a carnal practice that led to contentions. The same word *contentions* and a similar word *strife* are both used by Paul as he enumerates the works of the flesh (Galatians 5:20). (It is interesting that George Washington also warned the United States about political parties and factions for the same reason.)

One objection to this rule is that there are many members in the body of Christ with different ministries and that each denomination or movement is designed to show one particular part of the whole Gospel message. The apostle Paul certainly describes the body of Christ this way in no uncertain terms, even taking time to explain that the ear cannot say to the eye that it has no place in the body or the foot to the hand. The whole purpose of his exhortation, though, was to establish the unity of believers within their giftings.

> For by one Spirit are we all baptized into one body, whether we be Jews or Gentiles, whether we be bond or free; and have been all made to drink into one Spirit. (1 Corinthians 12:13 KJV)

> That there should be no schism in the body; but that the members should have the same care one for another. (1 Corinthians 12:25 KJV)

There can be little doubt that the Corinthian Christians had experienced the power of the Gospel in the new birth. Their lives had changed by the Spirit, but here Paul calls them carnal. He gives an explanation for the charge.

> For ye are yet carnal: for whereas there is among you envying, and strife, and divisions, are ye not carnal, and walk as men? For while one saith, I am of Paul; and another, I am of Apollos; are ye not carnal? Who then is Paul, and who is Apollos, but ministers by whom ye believed, even as the Lord gave to every man? I have planted, Apollos watered; but God gave the increase. So then neither is he that planteth any thing, neither he that water-

> eth; but God that giveth the increase. Now he that planteth and he that watereth are one: and every man shall receive his own reward according to his own labour. For we are labourers together with God: ye are God's husbandry, ye are God's building. (1 Corinthians 3:3–9 KJV)

Paul makes plain that ministers and spiritual leaders are simply men called to a specific work and labor of love. As much as people love hero worship, it has no place in the church. It is not the one that plants or the one who waters, says Paul, but God who gives the increase. As each one will stand before God, each one will be rewarded according to his own labor—but we all belong to God.

2. Economic differences

Jesus spoke plainly that the poor are always with us.

> My brethren, do not hold your faith in our glorious Lord Jesus Christ with an attitude of personal favoritism. For if a man comes into your assembly with a gold ring and dressed in fine clothes, and there also comes in a poor man in dirty clothes, and you pay special attention to the one who is wearing the fine clothes, and say, "You sit here in a good place," and you say to the poor man, "You stand over there, or

> sit down by my footstool," have you not made distinctions among yourselves, and become judges with evil motives? (James 2:1–10 NKJV)

Jesus did not come to bring economic equity, though you may be hearing much about that in our current political theater. What mattered to the Lord is how we react to the poor.

When Paul made himself known to the apostles in Jerusalem, they encouraged him to *remember the poor.* Paul himself also felt strongly to encourage the church in that direction. The point James was making is that such favoritism for the rich smacks of judgments, of distinctions between people of different economic status. This was divisive and so not to be tolerated in the church.

Solomon speaks to this issue in the story of a poor man who saved a city.

> There was a little city, and few men within it; and there came a great king against it, and besieged it, and built great bulwarks against it: Now there was found in it a poor wise man, and he by his wisdom delivered the city; yet no man remembered that same poor man. Then said I, Wisdom is better than strength: nevertheless the poor man's wisdom is despised, and his words are not heard. (Ecclesiastes 9:14–16 KJV)

Jesus reminded His disciples of this same principle in the account of the widow's mites. The amount was not important at all but the heart of giving, even out of lack. We express this when we say, "It's the thought that counts!"

3. Doctrinal differences

Everyone has an opinion or an interpretation. Though the Scripture is written in clear language, it should not surprise anyone that people from different backgrounds, cultures, or languages should interpret it differently in some instances, even applying it to their own culture. More than this, Paul uses the illustration of the vegetarian as an example of the weak brother who only eats vegetables. This could easily be interpreted against the background of a city as cosmopolitan as Corinth where the very best butcher shops adjoined temples where sacrifices to idols were made on a daily basis. This became a stumbling block to many, even to the point of contention within the church.

Paul deals with this issue with three main observations. First, that to eat or not eat does not carry any special weight with God. Neither does worship on one day or another.

> But meat commendeth us not to God: for neither, if we eat, are we the better; neither, if we eat not, are we the worse. But take heed lest by any means this liberty of yours become a stumblingblock to them that are weak. For if any man see thee which hast knowledge sit at meat in the idol's temple,

> shall not the conscience of him which is weak be emboldened to eat those things which are offered to idols; And through thy knowledge shall the weak brother perish, for whom Christ died? (1 Corinthians 8:8–11 KJV)

Secondly, as a corollary, Paul emphasizes that the relationship with the brother takes precedence over any other consideration. The brother who is weak in the faith, perhaps weak in the knowledge of the Scriptures or the grace of God, is not to be received into arguments. They are to be allowed to follow their own conscience in these matters.

> Him that is weak in the faith receive ye, but not to doubtful disputations. For one believeth that he may eat all things: another, who is weak, eateth herbs. Let not him that eateth despise him that eateth not; and let not him which eateth not judge him that eateth: for God hath received him. (Romans 14:1–3 KJV)

Jesus makes the same point a little differently when he declared, "The life is more than meat, and the body I more than raiment" (Luke 12:23 KJV). Thirdly, regardless of the issue, when a person follows their conscience in their own patterns of life, they do so with honor and thankfulness to God. They are, however, to be fully persuaded in their own mind. This is a maturing process and beyond any reasonable doubt includes the new convert as well as the experienced faithful.

> One man esteemeth one day above another: another esteemeth every day alike. Let every man be fully persuaded in his own mind. 6 He that regardeth the day, regardeth it unto the Lord; and he that regardeth not the day, to the Lord he doth not regard it. He that eateth, eateth to the Lord, for he giveth God thanks; and he that eateth not, to the Lord he eateth not, and giveth God thanks. (Romans 14:5–6 KJV)

What is not acceptable, Paul urges, is discord, dissensions, and factions. These are listed with all the other fleshly works of the sinful nature. People who live like that, Paul says, *will not inherit the kingdom of God.*

> The acts of the sinful nature are obvious: sexual immorality, impurity and debauchery; idolatry and witchcraft; hatred, *discord,* jealousy, fits of rage, selfish ambition, *dissensions, factions* and envy; drunkenness, orgies, and the like. I warn you, as I did before, that those who live like this will not inherit the kingdom of God. (Galatians 5:19–21 NIV, italics mine)

4. Natural differences

Here are differences that are not merely differences of opinion or interpretation, nor differences of social standing, nor differences in leadership.

> The body is a unit, though it is made up of many parts; and though all its parts are many, they form one body. So it is with Christ. For we were all baptized by one Spirit into one body-whether Jews or Greeks, slave or free-and we were all given the one Spirit to drink. (1 Corinthians 12:12–13 NIV)

Once again, the apostle Paul makes emphasis on the point that there are many members in the body, but only one body. In this case, he notes Jews and Greeks as well as slaves and freemen.

In his letter to the Colossians, he takes it a step further.

> Lie not one to another, seeing that ye have put off the old man with his deeds; And have put on the new man, which is renewed in knowledge after the image of him that created him: Where there is neither Greek nor Jew, circumcision nor uncircumcision, Barbarian, Scythian, bond nor free: but Christ is all, and in all. (Colossians 3:9–11 KJV)

And then another step further in his letter to the Galatians to include gender distinctions.

> There is neither Jew nor Greek, there is neither bond nor free, there is neither male nor female: for ye are all one in Christ Jesus. (Galatians 3:28 KJV)

This was not to deny the distinctiveness of nationality, social status, or gender but to simply make the point that all are in Christ. The word *Gentile* is a synonym for Greek, meaning any non-Jew. The fact is, scientifically, that there is one race—the human race, *Homo sapiens*—since biologically all peoples can interbreed. Biblically, we understand that all men and women descended from Adam and Eve with all the variations established within their genomes. The most obvious differences in various people groups are languages, skin color, and the basic features of hair and face. Skin color depends on the level of melanin, a pigment in the skin, and can be anywhere between almost pure white to pure black, but mostly shades of brown.

Here is the conclusion. God has created an incredible variety of everything—animal, vegetable, and mineral. There are about ten thousand species of birds, about the same number of species of fern and the list goes on. Just so, his church, his people, from *every nation, and kindred, and tongue, and people* (Revelation 14:6) share that same amazing creation variety, but they are still one church. The

Scriptures forbid me to separate myself from any of them. Paul puts it succinctly:

> You, then, why do you judge your brother? Or why do you look down on your brother? For we will all stand before God's judgment seat. It is written: "'As surely as I live,' says the Lord, 'every knee will bow before me; every tongue will confess to God.'" So then, each of us will give an account of himself to God. Therefore let us stop passing judgment on one another. Instead, make up your mind not to put any stumbling block or obstacle in your brother's way. (Romans 14:10–13)

Prayer

Father, you have given life and breath to all living. You have done this by your gracious hand. I am not your counselor or advisor to ask why you have done it this way, or to make suggestions or changes. I am simply one of your own. Forgive me when I have made judgments about my brother that I have neither the right nor ability to make. In Jesus's name. Amen.

The Prophet, the Donkey, and the Lion

> So he offered upon the altar which he had made in Bethel the fifteenth day of the eighth month, even in the month which he had devised of his own heart; and ordained a feast unto the children of Israel: and he offered upon the altar, and burnt incense.
>
> —1 Kings 12:33

In this short verse is the total condemnation of an entire religious system—its ordinances, its priesthood, and its origin. From beginning to end, it was an unmitigated disaster that resulted in the annihilation of ten tribes of Israel, the so-called lost tribes of Israel.

It is a common thing in nearly all cultures to see a business or trade move from father to son. The father gets older, becomes incapacitated, or dies. The son(s) or daughter(s), singly, or together, inherit the business or trade and all that comes with it. Even ministries have passed from father to son with varied results. It is often difficult for the new head of any successful program to be what the father or previous leader was, to fill their shoes so to speak. In a political sense, following a popular leader at any level is difficult at best and impossible at worst, but this scenario plays out in thousands of ways in countless similar situations every day.

Such was the case following the death of Solomon, arguably the greatest king of all Israel. His son, Rehoboam, was simply not a Solomon. The issue was a grassroots movement of an entire populace that had carried Solomon's grand building projects and heavy administrative infrastructure on their backs. Though they were loyal to both Solomon and his heir to the throne, they pled their case for tax and labor relief. Their spokesman was a former exile named Jereboam. This same Jereboam had been placed in a high position by Solomon and was popular with the people, but a discovered plot to take the kingdom from Solomon had sent him into exile. Now, he is back. This is how they presented their case.

> Thy father made our yoke grievous: now therefore make thou the grievous service of thy father, and his heavy yoke which he put upon us, lighter, and we will serve thee. (1 Kings 12:4 KJV)

Asking for three days to confer with his advisors, Reheboam sought counsel from the old school advisors that helped direct policy with Solomon. He listened carefully and respectfully but was determined to place his own mark on the kingdom. Finally, he consented to the advice of the young men he had grown up with rather than the wise counsel of the elders. So he answered the people roughly.

> And now whereas my father did lade you with a heavy yoke, I will add to your yoke: my father hath chastised you with whips, but I will chastise you with scorpions. (1 Kings 12:11 KJV)

The answer from the people was entirely predictable. They were more than tired of a strong centralized government that had preferred interests to Jerusalem over the rest of the country.

> So when all Israel saw that the king hearkened not unto them, the people answered the king, saying, What portion have we in David? neither have we inheritance in the son of Jesse: to your tents, O Israel: now see to thine own house, David. So Israel departed unto their tents. (1 Kings 12:16 KJV)

Plainly stated, they went home. Reheboam apparently did not get the full import of all this and went with his tax collector, Adoram, to receive taxes as usual. Adoram was stoned to death and Reheboam barely escaped with his life. The people of these ten tribes brought Jereboam back into the picture and promptly made him king.

> And it came to pass, when all Israel heard that Jeroboam was come again, that they sent and called him unto the congregation, and made him king over all Israel: there was none that followed the house of David, but the tribe of Judah only. (1 Kings 12:20 KJV)

Reheboam gathered an army of 180,000 fighting men to march against Jereboam and the rebel Israelites. To his credit, when rebuked by the Lord through the prophet Shemaiah, Reheboam called off his war and sent his soldiers home, having to be content with being King of Judah only.

"What advantage then hath the Jew?" the apostle Paul asks in his letter to the Romans (Romans 3:1). After seeing Paul demonstrate that all men are sinners, some may be tempted to say, "None! There is no advantage because all have sinned!" But Paul goes on rather unexpectedly to say: "Much every way: chiefly, because that unto them were committed the oracles of God" (Romans 3:2 KJV).

And that was the sticking point for Jereboam in establishing his new kingdom. The law and the prophets belonged to all Israel, all the children of Abraham through Isaac, Jacob, and Joseph. The law and the prophets spoke with one voice: "Hear, O Israel: The Lord our God is one Lord" (Deuteronomy 6:4 KJV).

Along with their clear understanding of monotheism, it was also plain that God had anointed the sons of Levi as the priesthood and the temple in Jerusalem as the one holy place of sacrifice. This was a torment to Jereboam as he reasoned it out in his mind.

> And Jeroboam said in his heart, Now shall the kingdom return to the house of David: If this people go up to do sacrifice in the house of the Lord at Jerusalem, then shall the heart of this people turn again unto their lord, even unto Rehoboam king of Judah, and they shall kill me, and go again to Rehoboam king of Judah. (1 Kings 12:26–27 KJV)

After counsel, Jeroboam established two cities, Dan and Bethel, as centers of worship. He had sculpted two golden calves, one for each city, and declared, "It is too much for you to go up to Jerusalem: behold thy gods, O Israel, which brought thee up out of the land of Egypt" (1 Kings 12:28 KJV).

Perhaps no one remembered the account of the golden calf fashioned by Aaron at the foot of Mt. Sinai, or perhaps no one was reading the Scriptures. Adding sin to sin, Jeroboam populated the high places and worship cities with a priesthood comprised of "the lowest of the people, which were not of the sons of Levi" (1 Kings 12:31). Further, he established holy days similar to those ordered by the Scriptures and took it upon himself to offer sacrifices himself, making himself priest and king.

Jeroboam and the entire religious system stand condemned as he left a worship that was divinely authorized and embraced rituals, services, and ceremonies completely of his own imagination. It is here that God intervenes in the form of an anonymous prophet from what is now called the Southern Kingdom or Judah.

> And, behold, there came a man of God out of Judah by the word of the Lord unto Bethel: and Jeroboam stood by the altar to burn incense. (1 Kings 13:1 KJV)

As King Jereboam stood by the altar, the Word of the Lord came forth from the anonymous prophet against the false altar:

> O altar, altar, thus saith the Lord; Behold, a child shall be born unto the house of David, Josiah by name; and upon thee shall he offer the priests of the high places that burn incense upon thee, and men's bones shall be burnt upon thee. And he gave a sign the same day, saying, This is the sign which the Lord hath spoken; Behold, the altar shall be rent, and the ashes that are upon it shall be poured out. (1 Kings 13:2–3 KJV)

Two amazing things are provided in this account. Firstly, that a future king from the true house of David would desecrate the false altar by burning men's bones upon it and the king's name would be Josiah! Secondly, the sign that this was indeed true prophecy was provided on the spot, the altar would be destroyed, split open, and its ashes poured out.

Then, three supernatural events happened in rapid sequence. Not surprisingly, King Jeroboam raised his hand against the prophet and ordered him seized. As he did, his hand withered up and could not be drawn back again. At the same time, the altar split and poured out ash. With his hand withered against the man of God, King Jereboam quickly pleaded for mercy and as the unknown prophet prayed, the king's hand was restored to normal.

No doubt stunned by this powerful demonstration right in front of all the people, officials, and priests alike, the king reverted to what he knew and was comfortable with. He invited the unnamed prophet to dinner and a reward. This invitation, however, was declined with an odd but very specific explanation.

> And the man of God said unto the king, If thou wilt give me half thine house, I will not go in with thee, neither will I eat bread nor drink water in this place: For so was it charged me by the word of the Lord, saying, Eat no bread, nor drink water, nor turn again by the same way that thou camest. So he went another way, and returned not by the way that he came to Bethel. (1 Kings 13:8–10 KJV)

The instructions from the Lord were unyielding and plain to the prophet, so he was unmoved by the king's offer. Having given the word of the Lord, his task was nearly completed. He had only to return home now by a different route.

We may marvel at the earthshaking events regarding the house of Israel and we may stand amazed at the acts of God in relation to his people. Still, as we consider what happened next, it is important for us to remember that these events were written for us, for our admonition, for our warning.

As might be expected, there were still prophets living in the northern kingdom. One such elderly prophet was told by his sons of the strange events in Bethel that day and of the strange unknown prophet who brought the Word of the Lord against the altar and the king. Without hesitation, he rode out after the prophet when he learned that his sons had seen the direction he had traveled from Bethel. Finding him beside the road resting under an oak, he invited him to come to his own house but received the same answer given to the king. He could not eat bread, drink water, or return home by the same route. But the older prophet was insistent.

> I am a prophet also as thou art; and an angel spake unto me by the word of the Lord, saying, Bring him back with thee into thine house, that he may eat bread and drink water. (1 Kings 13:18)

The Scriptures are plain that the older prophet had lied to him. Apparently believing the lie, the unnamed prophet followed him home for food and drink. In an amazing twist, as they sat at the table.

> As they sat at the table, that the word of the Lord came unto the prophet that brought him back: And he cried unto the man of God that came from Judah, saying, Thus saith the Lord, Forasmuch as thou hast disobeyed the mouth of the Lord, and hast not kept the commandment which the Lord thy God commanded thee, But camest back, and hast eaten bread and drunk water in the place, of the which the Lord did say to thee, Eat no bread, and drink no water; thy carcase shall not come unto the sepulchre of thy fathers. (1 Kings 13:20–22 KJV)

Whether our unnamed prophet believed this new twist or not, we have no way of knowing. Following what must have been a rather strained meal and fellowship, the old prophet gave him his own donkey for the remainder of his travel home. With the dire promise hanging over his head that his body would not make it home to the sepulchers of his fathers, the prophet took his leave.

On the way, however, he encountered a lion and was killed. Men passing by on the road saw such a strange sight, a lion, a donkey, and the body of a man. As strange as that was, even more strange was the fact that the lion and the donkey were just standing there, unmoving! The lion had not eaten the carcass nor had he bothered the donkey.

The old prophet heard about this strange encounter and knew at once that it was the prophet who had disobeyed the Lord. He went immediately and retrieved the body, grieving over all that had happened, and buried the unnamed prophet in his own sepulcher. He even gave instructions to his sons to bury him at his death in the same grave with the other prophet.

Not all the questions raised by this account have answers that are immediately discernable, but since this account is for our edification, perhaps we can take a lesson or two.

> Now all these things happened unto them for ensamples: and they are written for our admonition, upon whom the ends of the world are come. (1 Corinthians 10:11 KJV)

As strange as it may seem to us for one prophet of God to lie to another prophet of God, that is exactly what happened. As to his motivation, we may never know. We do know that an *appeal to a higher power* is an effective tool in persuasion. But note two things in particular:

1. God is not a man, that he should lie; neither the son of man, that he should repent: hath he said, and shall he not do it? or hath he spoken, and shall he not make it good? (Numbers 23:19)

Whether we understand or not, God will speak only the truth. His servants, on the other hand, are men and as such prone to mistakes, hyperbole, and outright false claims.

2. But though we, or an angel from heaven, preach any other gospel unto you than that which we have preached unto you, let him be accursed. (Galatians 1:8 KJV)

The warnings from Scripture are plain concerning *messages* from men, angels, or other spirits.

> Let no one cheat you of your reward, taking delight in false humility and worship of angels, intruding into those things which he has not seen, vainly puffed up by his fleshly mind, 19 and not holding fast to the Head, from whom all the body, nourished and knit together by joints and ligaments, grows with the increase that is from God. (Colossians 2:18–19 NKJV)

We can trust the Lord in our personal relationship with Him, the Head of His church. Isaiah reminds us, "Cease ye from man, whose breath is in his nostrils: for wherein is he to be accounted of?" (Isaiah 2:22 KJV).

Paul again in the New Testament takes extra care that God's people do not show partiality in regard to ministers.

> Who then is Paul, and who is Apollos, but ministers by whom ye believed, even as the Lord gave to every man? I have planted, Apollos watered; but God gave the increase. So then neither is he that planteth any thing, neither he that watereth; but God that giveth the increase. (1 Corinthians 3:5–7 KJV)

We should take seriously the words of Jesus himself.

> And the sheep hear his voice: and he calleth his own sheep by name, and leadeth them out. And when he putteth forth his own sheep, he goeth before them, and the sheep follow him: for they know his voice.
> 5 And a stranger will they not follow, but will flee from him: for they know not the voice of strangers. (John 10:3–5 KJV)

Prayer

Father, *Thy word is a lamp unto my feet and a light unto my path*. By your Word, I can see where I am standing, but I can also see where I am going. Grant to me again the light of your Word. Forgive me when I turn again to lean on my own understanding, but direct my steps. I know I can trust you. In Jesus's name. Amen.

O Mine Enemy

> And Ahab said to Elijah, Hast thou found me, O mine enemy?
>
> —1 Kings 21:20

There are many accounts of villainy and treachery in the historical narrative of the Old Testament. Many would think that the *Holy Bible* should not give credence to these nefarious people but if we know anything of God, anything of his Word—we should know that God sees things as they really are. That is to say, God sees them not as they could be, or should be, or might be, but as they actually are in truth.

> That they may know from the rising of the sun, and from the west, that there is none beside me. I am the Lord, and there is none else. I form the light, and create darkness: I make peace, and create evil: I the Lord do all these things. (Isaiah 45:6–7 KJV)

> For the word of God is quick, and powerful, and sharper than any twoedged sword, piercing even to the dividing asunder of soul and spirit, and of the joints and marrow, and is a discerner of the thoughts and intents of the heart. Neither is there any creature that is not manifest in his sight: but all things are naked and opened unto the eyes of him with whom we have to do. (Hebrews 4:12–13 KJV)

In a fallen world, we might admit that *history is written by the winners*, but the Scriptures present an accurate account of these historical events.

Perhaps the most infamous of all these accounts concerned a king and a queen, Ahab and Jezebel. They ruled the northern kingdom, commonly called Israel. Their palace was in Samaria, north of Jerusalem, the capital city of the Southern Kingdom of Judah. Next to their palace, apparently right against the walls, was the vineyard of Naboth. Naboth seemed a quiet and harmless man, but all advances by King Ahab to purchase that plot of ground for an herb garden were rebuffed. The land was an inheritance from his fathers and Naboth was unwilling to sell for any price, money, or land. In a childish tantrum, King Ahab refused to eat and fell across his bed in despair and disappointment.

All of that was remedied by his scheming wife, Jezebel. She was soon plotting against Naboth and devised a scheme that worked to perfection. Having lifted Naboth high into the public eye by the elders and nobles, worthless men (sons of Belial) then lied against him, claiming blasphemy against God and the king. So effective was this treachery that Naboth was taken out and stoned by the people of his city. It was so successful that King Ahab went down to take the vineyard for himself. It was at this point that God entered the picture in the person of Elijah the prophet.

> And the word of the Lord came to Elijah the Tishbite, saying, Arise, go down to meet Ahab king of Israel, which is in Samaria: behold, he is in the vineyard of Naboth, whither he is gone down to possess it. And thou shalt speak unto him, saying, Thus saith the Lord, Hast thou killed, and also taken possession? And thou shalt speak unto him, saying, Thus saith the Lord, In the place where dogs licked the blood of Naboth shall dogs lick thy blood, even thine. (1 Kings 21:17–19)

There was more to the message because Ahab was not to bear the guilt alone.

> And of Jezebel also spake the Lord, saying, The dogs shall eat Jezebel by the wall of Jezreel. (1 Kings 21:23 KJV)

Elijah met King Ahab in the garden of Naboth. As expected, the meeting was not a friendly one.

> And Ahab said to Elijah, Hast thou found me, O mine enemy? And he answered, I have found thee: because thou hast sold thyself to work evil in the sight of the Lord. (1 Kings 21:20 KJV)

King Ahab was so shaken by the prophecy against him that he humbled himself before the Lord and was granted a reprieve, but the sin and the damage were already accomplished and the judgment of the Lord rendered.

> But there was none like unto Ahab, which did sell himself to work wickedness in the sight of the Lord, whom Jezebel his wife stirred up. And he did very abominably in following idols, according to all things as did the Amorites, whom the Lord cast out before the children of Israel. And it came to pass, when Ahab heard those words, that he rent his clothes, and put sackcloth upon his flesh, and fasted, and lay in sackcloth, and went softly. (1 Kings 21:25–27 KJV)

It is very common in our world today to hear news about the horrible things people do to one another—the crimes they commit, the murders, the thefts. But more often than not, the punishment for those crimes goes unreported and the public at large can only hope that some kind of justice was imposed. This is especially true in our smaller communities that lack the facilities and resources of the larger cities.

> Because the sentence against an evil work is not executed speedily, therefore the heart of the sons of men is fully set in them to do evil. (Ecclesiastes 8:11–12 NKJV)

In this case, the judgment against King Ahab was accomplished three years later. The judgment against Queen Jezebel was delayed for about fourteen years. It is an important part of the story that is often overlooked. The beginning of the end started like this.

> And it came to pass in the third year, that Jehoshaphat the king of Judah came down to the king of Israel. (1 Kings 22:2 KJV)

In all the world, at any given moment, there are high-level diplomatic missions taking place between countries. It might well be said that the more things change the more they stay the same. The royal visit of these two kings was an amazing contradiction in itself. Ahab was an idolater, Jehoshaphat a worshipper of the One True God. Frictions between Israel and their near neighbor, Syria, had been quiet and relatively uneventful for three years. Perhaps it was time to make a move and regain some lost land, particularly the strategic city of Ramoth-Gilead. Strangely enough, Jehoshaphat agreed to a partnership in the venture.

> And he (Ahab) said unto Jehoshaphat, Wilt thou go with me to battle to Ramoth-gilead? And Jehoshaphat said to the king of Israel, I am as thou art, my people as thy people, my horses as thy horses. (1 Kings 22:4 KJV)

To us in this modern age, we might learn the lesson of the yoke.

> Be ye not unequally yoked together with unbelievers: for what fellowship hath righteousness with unrighteousness? and what communion hath light with darkness? And what concord hath Christ with Belial? or what part hath he that believeth with an infidel? And what agreement hath the temple of God with idols? for ye are the temple of the living God; as God hath said, I will dwell in them, and walk in them; and I will be their God, and they shall be my people. Wherefore come out from among them, and be ye separate, saith the Lord, and touch not the unclean thing; and I will receive you, And will be a Father unto you, and ye shall be my sons and daughters, saith the Lord Almighty. (2 Corinthians 6:14–18 KJV)

There was only one stipulation that Jehoshaphat brought into the discussion—that a prophet of God would be inquired of before setting out on this venture. King Ahab already had four hundred so-called prophets proclaiming a glorious conclusion, a God-given victory, a retaking of Ramoth-Gilead. "Go up!" they declared unanimously. One of their number, Zedekiah, actually produced iron horns and declared that the king would push out the Syrians from Ramoth. King Ahab was hesitant to call the one known prophet of God, Micaiah because, as he said in effect, "he never has anything good to say about me."

Still, Micaiah was brought before the kings to give a word from the Lord. Those that brought him to the kings urged him to not make a scene, to agree with the other four hundred prophets. Micaiah's response was simply that he would speak to the kings what God spoke to him, no more, no less.

The moment came for Micaiah to speak before the kings. What he spoke was exactly what the four hundred prophets had spoken!

> Go, and prosper: for the Lord shall deliver
> it into the hand of the king. (KJV)

There must have been a great collective sigh of relief from the four hundred prophets. Interestingly enough, it was King Ahab himself who perceived that what was spoken was not the Word of the Lord!

> And the king said unto him, How many times shall I adjure thee that thou tell me nothing but that which is true in the name of the Lord?

It was then that Micaiah delivered the message from God, the true word.

> I saw all Israel scattered upon the hills, as sheep that have not a shepherd: and the Lord said, These have no master: let them return every man to his house in peace.

The vision had two implications. King Ahab was going to his death, and the taking of Ramoth-Gilead would not be successful. King Ahab thought that the prophecy was a personal affront and that Micaiah was biased against him.

Then, Micaiah spoke again. This time, he shared with everyone present what he had seen in the Spirit. The death of Ahab was already prophesied, but there was some question about how was it to be accomplished. One spirit was commissioned by the Lord to be a lying spirit to the four hundred prophets of Ahab. It worked. All four hundred prophets of King Ahab heard the same thing, which said, "Go up! God will deliver it into your hands!" But they were deceived!

What happened next confirmed Micaiah's description of the spiritual events. Zedekiah, the one of the four hundred who had made iron horns, came to Micaiah and slapped his face.

> Which way went the Spirit of the Lord from me to speak unto thee?

Perhaps more than any time in their lives, these prophets, bought and paid for by the king, had heard a real message, a spiritual message—and it was confirmed by them all! Micaiah, the lone holdout, was sent to prison to await the outcome, but that outcome was never in doubt.

> And Micaiah said, If thou return at all in peace, the Lord hath not spoken by me.

Few scriptural accounts give rise to as many questions like this one. Some would ask if God had lied in this particular case. His methods of working his will in this case certainly seem out of the ordinary. An observation from Job can help us understand some of the supernatural workings of God.

> Behold, he withholdeth the waters, and they dry up: also he sendeth them out, and they overturn the earth. With him is strength and wisdom: the deceived and the deceiver are his. (Job 12:15–16)

The point is that God uses the waters in two ways—he holds them back, or he releases them in all their destructive power. Likewise, he holds both the deceived and the deceiver in his hands. Since both wisdom and power are his nature, he accomplishes his perfect will with any number of strategies. In the Book of Exodus, we read of Pharaoh's heart being hardened in three ways: his heart was hardened (neutral), Pharaoh hardened his heart, and God hardened Pharaoh's heart. From the context, it can be understood that all three of these things were happening at once. From the New Testament, we understand why and how deception comes.

> Because they received not the love of the truth, that they might be saved. And for this cause God shall send them strong delusion, that they should believe a lie. (2 Thessalonians 2:10–11 KJV)

> For the time will come when they will not endure sound doctrine; but after their own lusts shall they heap to themselves teachers, having itching ears; And they shall turn away their ears from the truth, and shall be turned unto fables. (2 Timothy 4:3–4 KJV)

From *Reason in the Balance* by Phillip E. Johnson, he says, "A person or a society that ignores the Creator is ignoring the most important part of reality, and to ignore reality is to be irrational."

It seems plain that to turn from truth is to turn to deception. From the biblical account of Ahab and Jehoshaphat, we see that they were determined to go their own way, regardless of the dire warnings from Micaiah. Knowing the warning, King Ahab added another deceit to avoid the coming judgment. It was determined that Ahab would go into battle disguised as a common warrior, but Jehoshaphat would go into battle in all his royal apparel.

As the battle commenced, the King of Syria instructed his captains to only go after the king of Israel. As his captains pressed hard against Jehoshaphat, he cried out and the Syrians realized that he was not the king and turned away. But another Syrian soldier shot an arrow in the chance that it would hit an enemy. It hit Ahab in a weak spot in his armor, a connecting piece, and he was mortally wounded. The word came that the battle was lost and the combined armies of Israel and Judah retreated in defeat, every man returning to his home just as the prophet had said.

But that was not the end of the story. King Ahab died and was buried in Samaria, but the account includes the fact that they washed his blood out of the chariot at the pool of Samaria, the exact place that Naboth had been stoned. The prophesied judgment upon Jezebel was also accomplished exactly as foretold. Thrown from her window on the wall of Jezreel and trampled by horses, the dogs left little to bury.

> And when Jehu was come to Jezreel, Jezebel heard of it; and she painted her face, and tired her head, and looked out at a window. And as Jehu entered in at the gate, she said, Had Zimri peace, who slew his master? And he lifted up his face to the window, and said, Who is on my side?

> who? And there looked out to him two or three eunuchs. And he said, Throw her down. So they threw her down: and some of her blood was sprinkled on the wall, and on the horses: and he trode her under foot. And when he was come in, he did eat and drink, and said, Go, see now this cursed woman, and bury her: for she is a king's daughter. And they went to bury her: but they found no more of her than the skull, and the feet, and the palms of her hands. (2 Kings 9:30–35 KJV)

So, in every point, the word of the Lord came to pass exactly as prophesied.

Prayer

Gracious Father, keep me from making unequal yokes for myself by joining into foolishness. Let me serve you with the freedom you have given me in Christ. In his name. Amen.

THE DEATH OF EZEKIEL'S WIFE

> Also the word of the Lord came unto me, saying, Son of man, behold, I take away from thee the desire of thine eyes with a stroke.
>
> —Ezekiel 24:15–18

The loss of a spouse, say the professional counselors, is one of the most heartrending sessions in all of counseling. The proliferation of grief counselors in this modern age is certainly interesting, but most will admit that having family and friends in your support during any difficult time will generally have close to the same positive effect. In spite of the abrupt life change, the loss will still hurt, you will still remember, and you will continue to be you. Though the prophet Ezekiel was warned of the coming loss of his wife, even an expected death is still a loss and still comes as a shock. This certainly had to be true of Ezekiel in his particular circumstances.

Nebuchadnezzar and the kingdom of Babylon ruled most of the known world in 597 BC. A major victory at Carchemish in 605 BC established them as a world power and the defeat of Egypt and the tiny country of Israel confirmed their position. Israel was subjected to tribute like many other nations under the Babylonian thumb, but they were an independent people whose God was the God of the whole earth. They simply could not imagine any role involving servitude. Even by the time of Christ, they responded to His claim that the truth would set them free by declaring, "We be Abraham's seed, and were never in bondage to any man: how sayest thou, Ye shall be made free?" (John 8:33).

Obviously, that was not true. At that very moment, they were under Roman rule. The sins of Israel had more than once in their history brought them into subjection to other nations. It was true again when Ezekiel with roughly ten thousand other skilled Israelites was taken captive and transported to the River Chebar in Babylon. They followed the captivity of Daniel, Hananiah, Mishael, and Azariah (known in Babylon by their Babylonian names as Belteshazzar, Shadrach, Meshach, and Abednego) a few years before. In spite of certain prophets declaring that Babylon would fall within two years, the prophet Jeremiah foretold a seventy-year captivity and advised the captives in a letter to settle in the new land. Life goes on.

> Thus saith the Lord of hosts, the God of Israel, unto all that are carried away captives, whom I have caused to be carried away from Jerusalem unto Babylon; Build ye houses, and dwell in them; and plant gardens, and eat the fruit of them; Take ye wives, and beget sons and daughters;

> and take wives for your sons, and give your daughters to husbands, that they may bear sons and daughters; that ye may be increased there, and not diminished. And seek the peace of the city whither I have caused you to be carried away captives, and pray unto the Lord for it: for in the peace thereof shall ye have peace. (Jeremiah 29:4–7 KJV)

In spite of their circumstances, things could have been worse. Then, if the death of Ezekiel's wife was not bad enough, God's instructions on how he was to respond seemed impossible.

> Yet neither shalt thou mourn nor weep, neither shall thy tears run down. Forbear to cry, make no mourning for the dead, bind the tire of thine head upon thee, and put on thy shoes upon thy feet, and cover not thy lips, and eat not the bread of men. So I spake unto the people in the morning: and at even my wife died; and I did in the morning as I was commanded. (Ezekiel 24:15–18 KJV)

Forbidden all the cultural norms for grieving, Ezekiel did as God commanded. There are two quick lessons here. First, that God does not require what he does not supply.

> There hath no temptation (trial) taken you but such as is common to man: but God is faithful, who will not suffer you to be tempted above that ye are able; but will with the temptation also make a way to escape, that ye may be able to bear it. (1 Corinthians 10:13 KJV)

This is not an escape from a trial, but a way through the trial. There can be no doubt that God enabled Ezekiel to fulfill his command.

Secondly, it is pretty much impossible to separate our daily lives from the spiritual. Like all the prophets, such as Hosea, Ezekiel's personal life and fate were inextricably linked with his calling. Not everyone is called to the prophetic office, but the call to serve Christ is to separate from the world, and as such "all that will live godly in Christ Jesus shall suffer persecution" (2 Timothy 3:12).

Ezekiel has often been called *the illustrated prophet* because many of the things he did were not only prophetic but also physical illustrations to the children of Israel. And this was no different. His demeanor following his wife's death had stirred the community and they demanded to know why he was acting in such a disturbing manner.

> And the people said unto me, Wilt thou not tell us what these things are to us, that thou doest so? (Ezekiel 24:19 KJV)

Ezekiel's answer was quick and powerful. It began with the claim that what he was about to deliver was the word of the Lord.

> Then I answered them, The word of the Lord came unto me, saying, Speak unto the house of Israel, *Thus saith the Lord God; Behold, I will profane my sanctuary, the excellency of your strength, the desire of your eyes, and that which your soul pitieth;* and your sons and your daughters whom ye have left shall fall by the sword. And ye shall do as I have done: ye shall not cover your lips, nor eat the bread of men. And your tires shall be upon your heads, and your shoes upon your feet: ye shall not mourn nor weep; but ye shall pine away for your iniquities, and mourn one toward another. Thus Ezekiel is unto you a sign: according to all that he hath done shall ye do: and when this cometh, ye shall know that I am the Lord God. (Ezekiel 24:20–24 KJV, italics mine)

The apostle Paul in his letter to the Romans makes the strong irrefutable case that all men have sinned and come short of the glory of God. We are convinced of this, but when he asks what advantage has the Jew, we expect the answer to be none—they have no advantage. Instead, Paul says they have a great advantage! They have the oracles of

God—the Word of God! In Paul's prayer for them, he goes even further, declaring:

> Who are Israelites; to whom pertaineth the adoption, and the glory, and the covenants, and the giving of the law, and the service of God, and the promises; Whose are the fathers, and of whom as concerning the flesh Christ came, who is over all, God blessed for ever. Amen. (Romans 9:4–5 KJV)

However, these advantages would not overcome the basic sinfulness of all men. Israel became proud of itself. They were the chosen of God, and as one Jewish writer penned, the *goyim* (the nations) were as *spit in the bucket.* Forgetting that they were to be a blessing to all the world, they turned to religious pride. They gloried in their calling, in their ancestry as children of Abraham, and in their temple and priesthood ordained by God himself. They had been warned.

> Thus saith the Lord, Let not the wise man glory in his wisdom, neither let the mighty man glory in his might, let not the rich man glory in his riches: But let him that glorieth glory in this, that he understandeth and knoweth me, that I am the Lord which exercise lovingkindness, judgment, and righteousness, in the

> earth: for in these things I delight, saith the Lord. Behold, the days come, saith the Lord, that I will punish all them which are circumcised with the uncircumcised; Egypt, and Judah, and Edom, and the children of Ammon, and Moab, and all that are in the utmost corners, that dwell in the wilderness: for all these nations are uncircumcised, and all the house of Israel are uncircumcised in the heart. (Jeremiah 9:23–26)

So now the time had come. Listen carefully to God's warning given by the prophet Jeremiah, a contemporary of Ezekiel, who was commanded to stand in the gates of Jerusalem and declare the word of the Lord.

> Thus saith the Lord of hosts, the God of Israel, Amend your ways and your doings, and I will cause you to dwell in this place. Trust ye not in lying words, saying, The temple of the Lord, The temple of the Lord, The temple of the Lord, are these. For if ye throughly amend your ways and your doings; if ye throughly execute judgment between a man and his neighbour; If ye oppress not the stranger, the fatherless, and the widow, and shed not innocent blood in this place, neither walk after other gods to your hurt: Then will I cause

> you to dwell in this place, in the land that I gave to your fathers, for ever and ever. (Jeremiah 7:3–7 KJV)

Like the Israelites in the time of Samuel that foolishly looked superstitiously to the ark of the covenant to save them (*"it may save us;"* [1 Samuel 4:3]) rather than to the God of the covenant, so now they looked to the temple and their religion to save them rather than the God of the whole earth. Does it seem like the more things change the more they stay the same? How many millions have looked to their religion for salvation rather than a personal relationship with an Almighty God who loves them! While it is true that Israel had a national relationship with God, each individual in the nation was required to walk in the light of that relationship. Moses also warned the people about keeping that right relationship.

> Behold, I have taught you statutes and judgments, even as the Lord my God commanded me, that ye should do so in the land whither ye go to possess it. Keep therefore and do them; for this is your wisdom and your understanding in the sight of the nations, which shall hear all these statutes, and say, Surely this great nation is a wise and understanding people. For what nation is there so great, who hath God so nigh unto them, as the Lord our God is in all things that we call upon him

> for? And what nation is there so great, that hath statutes and judgments so righteous as all this law, which I set before you this day? Only take heed to thyself, and keep thy soul diligently, lest thou forget the things which thine eyes have seen, and lest they depart from thy heart all the days of thy life: but teach them thy sons, and thy sons' sons. (Deuteronomy 4:5–9 KJV)

So now, God is prepared to take from them that which they so greatly relied upon. The temple and all the religious activity involved there would cease. The very center of their pride and strength would be removed so that they would once again seek God himself.

> Thus saith the Lord God; Behold, I will profane my sanctuary, the excellency of your strength, the desire of your eyes, and that which your soul pitieth.

Ezekiel and the death of his wife were to become a sign to all Israel of what God was going to do. When the judgment was accomplished, they too were not to grieve over the loss, but realize that this was a righteous judgment from the Lord upon their faithlessness.

> Thus Ezekiel is unto you a sign: according to all that he hath done shall ye do: and when this cometh, ye shall know that I am

> the Lord God. Also, thou son of man, shall it not be in the day when I take from them their strength, the joy of their glory, the desire of their eyes, and that whereupon they set their minds, their sons and their daughters, That he that escapeth in that day shall come unto thee, to cause thee to hear it with thine ears? (Ezekiel 24:24–26)

As amazing as all of this is to our own ears, there is more. At the beginning of Ezekiel's ministry, he was forbidden to speak except when proclaiming the word of the Lord. As a result, at any moment that Ezekiel spoke aloud, everyone knew it was a word from the Lord. Because they were a rebellious house, as God said, the prophet was only allowed to speak prophetically.

> And I will make thy tongue cleave to the roof of thy mouth, that thou shalt be dumb (mute), and shalt not be to them a reprover: for they are a rebellious house. But when I speak with thee, I will open thy mouth, and thou shalt say unto them, Thus saith the Lord God; He that heareth, let him hear; and he that forbeareth, let him forbear: for they are a rebellious house. (Ezekiel 3:22–27)

Now, at the death of his wife, God explains to Ezekiel and the people that when the judgment is accomplished and the news comes to the captives, Ezekiel will be freed from that limitation and able to speak normally.

> In that day shall thy mouth be opened to him which is escaped, and thou shalt speak, and be no more dumb (mute): and thou shalt be a sign unto them; and they shall know that I am the Lord. (Ezekiel 24:27 KJV)

Exactly on time, the Scriptures record the moment Ezekiel's mouth was opened.

> And it came to pass in the twelfth year of our captivity, in the tenth month, in the fifth day of the month, that one that had escaped out of Jerusalem came unto me, saying, The city is smitten. Now the hand of the Lord was upon me in the evening, afore he that was escaped came; and had opened my mouth, until he came to me in the morning; and my mouth was opened, and I was no more dumb (mute). (Ezekiel 33:21–22 KJV)

Once again, Ezekiel was a sign that what God had declared he had accomplished.

> For as the rain cometh down, and the snow from heaven, and returneth not thither,

> but watereth the earth, and maketh it bring forth and bud, that it may give seed to the sower, and bread to the eater: So shall my word be that goeth forth out of my mouth: it shall not return unto me void, but it shall accomplish that which I please, and it shall prosper in the thing whereto I sent it. (Isaiah 55:10–11 KJV)

Prayer

Heavenly Father, we are moving through some strange times in our world. Much of it seems to be of our own making. Help us to remember that if we will humble ourselves, and pray, and turn from our wicked ways to seek your face—you will hear our prayer and heal our land.

Creation Implications

> For by him were all things created, that are in heaven, and that are in earth, visible and invisible, whether they be thrones, or dominions, or principalities, or powers: all things were created by him, and for him: And he is before all things, and by him all things consist.
>
> —Colossians 1:16–17 KJV

It was the work of the Old Testament priesthood to make a difference between the holy and the profane, or secular. During the time of Israel's captivity, the prophet Ezekiel hears and records these words from the Lord God Almighty.

> Her priests have violated my law, and have profaned mine holy things: they have put no difference between the holy and profane, neither have they shewed difference between the unclean and the clean, and have hid their eyes from my sabbaths, and I am profaned among them. (Ezekiel 22:26 KJV)

In the historical account provided in Genesis, we understand that God created this world in perfection. There was no sin, and thus there was no death. All of creation was in harmony with every other part of creation. Living things all had their place. God made the sky and filled it with birds. He made the oceans and filled them with sea creatures. He made the land and from it sprang living grasses and shrubs and trees, as well as the multitude of land creatures that ate the grasses, shrubs, and trees, including man. The amazing cycles of oxygen, carbon, nitrogen, and other essential elements that maintain life speak plainly that all of these things necessarily had to be in place at the same time. It is an example of what microbiologist Michael Behe called *irreducible complexity*. It is something so complex and interrelated that it would be impossible for them to form separately over time. They all needed to be in place from the beginning for any of it to work.

Because no one was there to witness this creation, the writer of Hebrews makes this pertinent observation.

> Through faith we understand that the worlds were framed by the word of God, so that things which are seen were not made of things which do appear. (Hebrews 11:3 KJV)

With our modern understanding of chemistry and the atomic world, as incomplete as it is, this statement seems remarkably accurate. No one has ever seen an electron and yet the substances we know, use, and study in our everyday lives are made by these invisible units as part of the basic building blocks of atoms. Even our own selves, as the psalmist declares, are "fearfully and wonderfully made" (Ps 139). Though we see the results of creation, it seems obvious that we cannot prove scientifically that the worlds were framed by the word of God. It remains a faith issue, just as it is for those who believe with all their heart that there is no God and this world simply formed itself.

In the beginning, there was nothing, and nothing exploded, bringing all matter and life into existence. That, too, is a faith statement. There was no observation, no witnesses to such an event and so must be taken on faith. It is a belief system. However, there are implications to any belief system. We talk glibly about blind faith, but that is not accurate. There needs to be a foundation, a background, even a history that provides a context for belief.

> A person or a society that ignores the Creator is ignoring the most important part of reality, and to ignore reality is to be irrational. (Phillip E. Johnson)

Creation implies ownership

> The earth is the Lord's, and the fulness thereof; the world, and they that dwell therein. For he hath founded it upon the seas, and established it upon the floods. (Psalm 24:12 KJV)

The phrase *the earth is the Lord's* was probably taken as an established fact in the minds of God's people, but we first see this phrase in Exodus 9 as God brought both hail and fire against the Egyptians as one of the ten plagues. It appears again in the Psalms (Psalms 89). The phrase is quoted by the apostle Paul (1 Corinthians 10:26 and 28) in his discourse concerning meat sacrificed to idols. That God owns what he created is explained in a different way in Psalms 50.

> For every beast of the forest is mine, and the cattle upon a thousand hills. I know all the fowls of the mountains: and the wild beasts of the field are mine. If I were hungry, I would not tell thee: for the world is mine, and the fulness thereof. (Psalm 50:10–12 KJV)

It is within this framework that we understand why God is called a *jealous* God, and why the image set up in the gate at Jerusalem (Ezekiel 8–10) was called the *image of jealousy*. The Ten Commandments remind us to *have no other gods before me.* Since all of these things are created and owned by God, it is his gracious hands that provide them and his hands only! This also gives meaning to the eighth commandment, "You shall not steal" (Exodus 20:15). God is firm on property rights, and the Law of Moses emphasized that all we obtain must be obtained lawfully. Even today, we have copyright laws and patent laws that recognize the rights of ownership and enforces penalties upon those who violate those laws.

> Thou art worthy, O Lord, to receive glory and honour and power: for thou hast created all things, and for thy pleasure they are and were created. (Revelation 4:11 KJV)

As a corollary, ownership also implies accountability. God has not only created all things, but they are created with a holy purpose. For instance, in the parable of the talents:

> For the kingdom of heaven is as a man travelling into a far country, who called his own servants, and delivered unto them his goods. (Matthew 25:14 KJV)

These were *his* servants and he delivered to them *his* goods for investment. They were accountable to him for their wise use of his goods. Their faithful and productive service was rewarded on the day of reckoning, or judgment, with, "Well done, good and faithful servant."

Likewise, God formed the world for habitation. It was populated not only with humans but also with an incredible variety of birds, fish, animals, insects, and an entire unseen world of microscopic creatures! These all had a purpose and fulfilled that purpose on the earth.

> For thus saith the Lord that created the heavens; God himself that formed the earth and made it; he hath established it, he created it not in vain, he formed it to be inhabited: I am the Lord; and there is none else. (Isaiah 45:18 KJV)

> God that made the world and all things therein, seeing that he is Lord of heaven and earth, dwelleth not in temples made with hands; Neither is worshipped with men's hands, as though he needed any thing, seeing he giveth to all life, and breath, and all things; And hath made of one blood all nations of men for to dwell on all the face of the earth, and hath determined the times before appointed, and the bounds of their habitation; That they should seek the Lord. (Acts 17:24–27 KJV)

Jesus confirmed the nature of God as Father, not just as Creator. The Father loves his children.

Creation implies complexity

> I will praise thee; for I am fearfully and wonderfully made: marvellous are thy works; and that my soul knoweth right well. (Psalm 139:14 KJV)

Though some may deny it, what we see in our world is design. This is *top down* engineering at its very best. You could have all the materials for a bridge placed on the bank of a river, but they would never organize into a bridge. There must be an idea, an intelligent design if you will, to bring the parts together in a structure that will actually span the river.

Like the mousetrap, it is an all-or-nothing unity. Though there are relatively few pieces to a mousetrap, if you take out a single piece, the whole thing becomes useless. We are back again to Behe's irreducible complexity. Behe emphasizes this complexity by stating further that in living "organisms, some parts are so important to the function of life that if they are missing, life stops."

Even Charles Darwin was well aware that the eye alone with its amazing complexity could not have formed by slow stages over eons of time. It was a valid objection to his entire theory, not to mention the fossil record that only revealed life forms as complete and individual from the beginning. (Another 150 years of fossil hunting still has the missing link missing.)

Life itself is supernatural. No one has been able to explain the origin of life from a naturalistic view. The origin of life by any other explanation than creation falls apart against the amazing complexity of life itself. Naturalistic theories of the origin of life finally fall into two categories: panspermia (that life was seeded on earth by aliens) and panpsychism (that all things physical like rocks and water have an internal life force).

Even our physical universe speaks of a complexity completely beyond the understanding of man.

> When I consider thy heavens, the work of thy fingers, the moon and the stars, which thou hast ordained; What is man, that thou art mindful of him? and the son of man, that thou visitest him? For thou hast made him a little lower than the angels, and hast crowned him with glory and honour. Thou madest him to have dominion over the works of thy hands; thou hast put all things under his feet: All sheep and oxen, yea, and the beasts of the field; The fowl of the air, and the fish of the sea, and whatsoever passeth through the paths of the seas. O Lord our Lord, how excellent is thy name in all the earth! (Psalm 8:3–9)

All of these things speak to a Creator God outside of time and space. They speak of a power that is inconceivable to the natural mind. As Paul the Apostle puts it:

> For the invisible things of him from the creation of the world are clearly seen, being understood by the things that are made, even his eternal power and Godhead; so that they are without excuse: Because that, when they knew God, they glorified him not as God, neither were thankful; but

> became vain in their imaginations, and their foolish heart was darkened. (Romans 1:20–21 KJV)

Creation implies maintenance

> Thou, even thou, art Lord alone; thou hast made heaven, the heaven of heavens, with all their host, the earth, and all things that are therein, the seas, and all that is therein, and thou preservest them all; and the host of heaven worshippeth thee. (Nehemiah 9:6 KJV)

> For in him we live, and move, and have our being. (Acts 17:28 KJV)

Nehemiah clearly understood that God was not only a Creator, but also a Sustainer. He preserves his creation. One of the accusations against the elders of Israel during the Babylonian captivity was that they really believed that God was absent from his creation, that he was an absentee landlord, so to speak, that he did not concern himself with the affairs of men. It was as if God gave the world a spin and left it on its own.

> Then said he unto me, The iniquity of the house of Israel and Judah is exceeding great, and the land is full of blood, and

> the city full of perverseness: for they say, The Lord hath forsaken the earth, and the Lord seeth not. (Ezekiel 9:9 KJV)

Our original text speaks to this very issue.

> For by him were all things created, that are in heaven, and that are in earth, visible and invisible, whether they be thrones, or dominions, or principalities, or powers: all things were created by him, and for him: <u>And he is before all things, and by him all things consist</u>. (Colossians 1:16–17)

The word *consist* implies a standing, a holding together, a continuing. Our very existence premised upon the will of God, his faithfulness, his plan, and his promise. Just as there was a beginning for our universe, there will be an end. This idea confounded many of the early philosophers who thought of the universe as eternal, without beginning or end. Even the famous physicist and mathematician Albert Einstein was unhappy with his theories because by extrapolating backward they pointed to a beginning. This sounded too much like creation to him and he tried to work around it, but unsuccessfully. From all this came the naturalistic theory of the Big Bang to explain the beginning in very natural terms without resorting to a Creator, or as one scientist put it, allowing "a Divine foot in the door."

> And, Thou, Lord, in the beginning hast laid the foundation of the earth; and the heavens are the works of thine hands: They shall perish; but thou remainest; and they all shall wax old as doth a garment; And as a vesture shalt thou fold them up, and they shall be changed: but thou art the same, and thy years shall not fail. (Hebrews 1:10–12 KJV)

Naturalistic scientists point to a *heat death* of the universe. That is, that according to the laws of thermodynamics, everything will eventually run down as all the energy drains out of it. These *laws* indicate that this is the way it will work without further energy placed into the system. The whole thing will simply run down and end up cold (very cold!) and dead. Of course, we are talking about billions of years as our sun uses up all its fuel and other suns die out as well. Humanity will be long gone before this happens, according to science.

The Scriptures, however, tell of a different ending. There will be a new heaven and a new earth.

> But the day of the Lord will come as a thief in the night; in the which the heavens shall pass away with a great noise, and the elements shall melt with fervent heat, the earth also and the works that are therein shall be burned up. Seeing then that all these things shall be dissolved, what man-

ner of persons ought ye to be in all holy conversation and godliness, Looking for and hasting unto the coming of the day of God, wherein the heavens being on fire shall be dissolved, and the elements shall melt with fervent heat? Nevertheless we, according to his promise, look for new heavens and a new earth, wherein dwelleth righteousness. (2 Peter 3:10–13 KJV)

And the angel which I saw stand upon the sea and upon the earth lifted up his hand to heaven, And sware by him that liveth for ever and ever, who created heaven, and the things that therein are, and the earth, and the things that therein are, and the sea, and the things which are therein, that there should be time no longer. (Revelation 10:5–6 KJV)

And God shall wipe away all tears from their eyes; and there shall be no more death, neither sorrow, nor crying, neither shall there be any more pain: for the former things are passed away. And he that sat upon the throne said, Behold, I make all things new. And he said unto me, Write: for these words are true and faithful. (Revelation 21:4–5 KJV)

The Faithful One who created us for his own purposes will likewise keep us until that day. As Paul the Apostle declared, "Nevertheless I am not ashamed: for I know whom I have believed, and am persuaded that he is able to keep that which I have committed unto him against that day" (2 Timothy 1:12).

Prayer

Wonderful Creator, how beautiful is that which you have made! How glorious in beauty and complexity is every living thing! Even the heavens declare your glory and power. Father, bring to us again not only the awe of your creation but also the splendor of your love and redemption in our individual lives. You alone are God!

FIVE KINGS IN A CAVE

Some of the very best-known historical accounts in Scripture have hidden *spiritual nuggets* either before or after the main text. This is called context. As someone has wisely pointed out: "Whenever you see a *therefore*, you should find out what it is there for!" While it is usually good hermeneutics to take the historical account at face value, we can remember the exhortation from the apostle Paul, which says, "These things happened to them as examples and were written down as warnings for us, on whom the fulfillment of the ages has come" (1 Corinthians 10:11 NIV).

Ask anyone about the sun not setting for a day and they will point you quickly to the account of Joshua's battle in Joshua 10. There is an interesting background to the account, but there was also an instructive incident following the victory.

Here is the background. God's promise to Abraham included basically three things: (1) a son (which we now know to have been Isaac), (2) a land (which we now know to be the land of Israel), and (3) a blessing that would encompass the whole world (which we now understand to be the Messiah, the Christ). This promise was repeated to Abraham at least six times, and at least one time, because Abraham was just not sure how God was going to do this, though he believed God explicitly. From the repetition of the promise in Genesis 15, Abraham began to understand the part about the land.

> In the same day the Lord made a covenant with Abram, saying, Unto thy seed have I given this land, from the river of Egypt unto the great river, the river Euphrates: The Kenites, and the Kenizzites, and the Kadmonites, And the Hittites, and the Perizzites, and the Rephaims, And the Amorites, and the Canaanites, and the Girgashites, and the Jebusites. (Genesis 15:18–21 KJV)

That the land was already occupied may have presented a problem in the mind of Abraham, but God explained that part as well.

> And he said unto Abram, Know of a surety that thy seed shall be a stranger in a land that is not theirs, and shall serve them; and they shall afflict them four hundred years; And also that nation, whom they shall serve, will I judge: and afterward shall they come out with great substance. And thou shalt go to thy fathers in peace; thou shalt be buried in a good old age. But in the fourth generation they shall come hither

> again: for the iniquity of the Amorites is not yet full. (Genesis 15:13–16 KJV)

Though it involved a four-hundred-year wait, the wait was balanced by the fact that they would have great wealth as they inherited the land. This promise was fulfilled exactly by their slavery in Egypt, the spoiling of Egypt as they left, the exodus itself led by Moses and the visible presence of God, and the miraculous taking of the land by Israel led by Joshua.

Several reasons for these four hundred years have been given by scribes, commentators, and philosophers over the intervening centuries, but God himself gives one of his purposes: "For the iniquity of the Amorites is not yet full."

How quickly we forget that *God so loved the world*! These Hittites, Amorites, Canaanites, Perizzites, Hivites, and Jebusites were all people groups that God loved and cherished, but as they turned from God, they had progressed in their wickedness. The Scriptures speak of child sacrifice, temple prostitution, idolatry, and all manner of religious perversions that were leading up to a time of judgment. Generations of these precious people came and went as God allowed time for repentance and change.

Though many individuals like Rahab may have turned to God, only the clan of Gibeon had made a treaty with Joshua of all the cities and peoples. Though that treaty was accomplished by deception, Joshua had committed to protection for the Gibeonites. Their explanation for the deception was simply and honestly given.

> Because it was certainly told thy servants, how that the Lord thy God commanded his servant Moses to give you all the land, and to destroy all the inhabitants of the land from before you, therefore we were sore afraid of our lives because of you, and have done this thing. (Joshua 9:24 KJV)

What happened then was entirely predictable.

> Now it came to pass, when Adoni-zedek king of Jerusalem had heard how Joshua had taken Ai, and had utterly destroyed it; as he had done to Jericho and her king, so he had done to Ai and her king; and how the inhabitants of Gibeon had made peace with Israel, and were among them; That they feared greatly, because Gibeon was a great city, as one of the royal cities, and because it was greater than Ai, and all the men thereof were mighty. (Joshua 10:1–4)

To no one's surprise, the king of Jerusalem (the Jebusites) called upon his threatened neighbors to form a coalition to reclaim Gibeon and resist the invading forces of Joshua.

> Come up unto me, and help me, that we may smite Gibeon: for it hath made peace with Joshua and with the children of Israel. Therefore the five kings of the

> Amorites, the king of Jerusalem, the king of Hebron, the king of Jarmuth, the king of Lachish, the king of Eglon, gathered themselves together, and went up, they and all their hosts, and encamped before Gibeon, and made war against it. (Joshua 10:4–5 KJV)

Under threat of annihilation, Gibeon sent messengers to Joshua for protection under the treaty. After an all-night march from Gilgal and a promise from God of complete victory, the armies of Israel came upon the five kings in force. And so began one of the greatest one-sided battles in history. This account stands in direct repudiation of those who believe that God gave the world a spin and then abdicated. He is not an absentee landlord.

Though the battle took place on the earth with physical combatants, the working of God Almighty is clearly seen. God is for Israel, and God fights for Israel.

> And the Lord discomfited them before Israel, and slew them with a great slaughter at Gibeon, and chased them along the way that goeth up to Beth-horon, and smote them to Azekah, and unto Makkedah. And it came to pass, as they fled from before Israel, and were in the going down to Beth-horon, that the Lord cast down great stones from heaven upon them unto Azekah, and they died: they were more

> which died with hailstones than they whom the children of Israel slew with the sword. (Joshua 10:10–11 KJV)

It was here at this point, as the battle was being fought that Joshua called for extra time to complete the victory.

> Then spake Joshua to the Lord in the day when the Lord delivered up the Amorites before the children of Israel, and he said in the sight of Israel, Sun, stand thou still upon Gibeon; and thou, Moon, in the valley of Ajalon. And the sun stood still, and the moon stayed, until the people had avenged themselves upon their enemies. Is not this written in the book of Jasher? So the sun stood still in the midst of heaven, and hasted not to go down about a whole day. And there was no day like that before it or after it, that the Lord hearkened unto the voice of a man: for the Lord fought for Israel. (Joshua 10:12–14)

Once again, the God who created time is in charge of time. God had provided four hundred years for the inhabitants of the land to make changes and come to repentance. Now, he provides extra time for a victory for his people, even stopping heaven and earth.

This command of time is seen again in the closing hours of the battle. Realizing that the battle was lost, the five kings fled and hid themselves in a cave. Unwillingly to interrupt the momentum of the battle, Joshua commanded these *kings* to be sealed in with stones and a guard set. Held securely in the cave, they could be dealt with later after the heat of battle had passed. Following the utter defeat of the enemy, Joshua came back to Makkedah and the captive kings.

> Then said Joshua, Open the mouth of the cave, and bring out those five kings unto me out of the cave. And they did so, and brought forth those five kings unto him out of the cave, the king of Jerusalem, the king of Hebron, the king of Jarmuth, the king of Lachish, and the king of Eglon. And it came to pass, when they brought out those kings unto Joshua, that Joshua called for all the men of Israel, and said unto the captains of the men of war which went with him, Come near, put your feet upon the necks of these kings. And they came near, and put their feet upon the necks of them. And Joshua said unto them, Fear not, nor be dismayed, be strong and of good courage: for thus shall the Lord do to all your enemies against whom ye fight. (Joshua 10:22–25 KJV)

What an amazing turn of events! When we understand the apostle Paul's instruction that "these things happened to them as examples," we can take a lesson.

For instance, we understand from the words of Jesus that "whosoever commits sin is the servant of sin" (John 8:34). Since "all have sinned" (Romans 3:23), all of us have *kings* in our lives that may rule and bring defeat into our lives. Here are a few Scriptural examples (though by no means exhaustive):

King Fear (nightmares, irrational fears, finances/health)

Fears, both rational and irrational, plague mankind. Chief among them is the fear of death, but the promise of Christ is to "deliver them who through fear of death were all their lifetime subject to bondage" (Hebrews 2:15). The fear of judgment or personal harm is a constant in the human experience. We all have faced fears of sickness, fears of financial devastation, a plethora of phobias and nightmares, and a thousand other fears common to man.

Job records his own experience, which says, "In thoughts from the visions of the night, when deep sleep falleth on men, Fear came upon me, and trembling, which made all my bones to shake" (Job 4:13–14 KJV). The promise of God is *fear not* because "God has not given us a spirit of fear, but of power and of love and of a sound mind" (2 Timothy 1:7 NKJV). Perhaps the most famous and most quoted of these promises is Psalm 23:4, which says, "Yea, though I walk through the valley of the shadow of death, I will fear no evil; for thou art with me."

King Lust

Though we often think of the word *lust* with sexual connotations, the meaning of the word is literally *the desire of the soul.* It is the disposition of the heart and can involve an overpowering desire without thought to the will of God or even common good sense. The intense desire for recognition, achievement, power, riches, or fame all comes under this heading. This is not from God but from within the soulish nature, the mind of man.

> Let no one say when he is tempted, "I am tempted by God"; for God cannot be tempted by evil, nor does He Himself tempt anyone. But each one is tempted when he is drawn away by his own desires and enticed. Then, when desire has conceived, it gives birth to sin; and sin, when it is full-grown, brings forth death. (James 1:13–15 NKJV)

Perhaps this is why Jesus taught us to pray to our Father, "thy will be done." It has been said that there are two kinds of people in the world, those who say, "Thy will be done" to a wonderful Heavenly Father, or those to whom the Father says, "Thy will be done." The gift of free will is a powerful thing.

King Pride

The sin of pride can take a million shapes, including the delusional form of religious pride. There is a natural pride, a natural joy in accomplishment. The sin of pride, however, has to do with arrogance and haughtiness.

> For everything in the world-the cravings of sinful man, the lust of his eyes and (pride of life) the boasting of what he has and does-comes not from the Father but from the world. The world and its desires pass away, but the man who does the will of God lives forever. (1 John 2:16–17 NIV)

Solomon recognized the dangers of this kind of presumption.

> In the day of prosperity be joyful, but in the day of adversity consider: God also hath set the one over against the other, to the end that man should find nothing after him. (Ecclesiastes 7:14 KJV)

King Unforgiveness

The Scriptures identify this *king* as a *root of bitterness* that comes with defiling power.

> Follow peace with all men, and holiness, without which no man shall see the Lord: Looking diligently lest any man fail of the grace of God; lest any root of bitterness springing up trouble you, and thereby many be defiled. (Hebrews 12:14–15 KJV)

We can again turn to the parables of Jesus and to the Lord's Prayer to understand the seriousness of an unforgiving spirit.

> Take heed to yourselves: If thy brother trespass against thee, rebuke him; and if he repent, forgive him. And if he trespass against thee seven times in a day, and seven times in a day turn again to thee, saying, I repent; thou shalt forgive him. (Luke 17:3–4 KJV)

> And forgive us our debts, as we forgive our debtors. (Matthew 6:12 KJV)

King Addiction

There are physical addictions that if not broken can destroy a person. There are also addictions to habits and ways of thinking. Just as a person can become addicted to drugs, there can be addictions to anger or other harmful emotions. These are physical carnal mindsets that are difficult or impossible to remove once put into place. The Scripture warns us: "He that is slow to anger is better than the mighty; and he that ruleth his spirit than he that taketh a city" (Proverbs 16:32 KJV).

How are these *kings* conquered? Are we just caught in a natural trap of mind and emotion that cannot be escaped?

> For though we walk in the flesh, we do not war after the flesh: (For the weapons of our warfare are not carnal, but mighty through God to the pulling down of strong holds;) Casting down imaginations, and every high thing that exalteth itself against the knowledge of God, and bringing into captivity every thought to the obedience of Christ. (2 Corinthians 10:3–5 KJV)

As in all of our trials and temptations, God has provided a way of escape.

> If ye then be risen with Christ, seek those things which are above, where Christ sitteth on the right hand of God. Set your affection on things above, not on things on the earth. For ye are dead, and your life is hid with Christ in God. When Christ, who is our life, shall appear, then shall ye also appear with him in glory. Mortify therefore your members which are upon

> the earth; fornication, uncleanness, inordinate affection, evil concupiscence, and covetousness, which is idolatry: For which things' sake the wrath of God cometh on the children of disobedience: In the which ye also walked some time, when ye lived in them. But now ye also put off all these; anger, wrath, malice, blasphemy, filthy communication out of your mouth. Lie not one to another, seeing that ye have put off the old man with his deeds; And have put on the new man, which is renewed in knowledge after the image of him that created him. (Colossians 3:1–10 KJV)

The promise of God given to Ezekiel is that he would provide a new heart and a new mind to those who turn to him. This is fulfilled in what we call *the new birth.* Jesus explained to Nicodemus, "You must be born again." Though we are granted a new life in Christ Jesus, we remain creatures of time. The idea of a person caught between two worlds is a difficult concept. Jesus explained to Nicodemus, "The wind bloweth where it listeth, and thou hearest the sound thereof, but canst not tell whence it cometh, and whither it goeth: so is every one that is born of the Spirit" (John 3:8 KJV).

Though we have an immediate deliverance from sin and its consequence, the work of the cross must become the way of the cross. This can be thought of as steps in a process: to be (creaturehood), to become (sonship), to share (responsibility), and to reign (as kings and priests in eternity). We must walk our lives carefully and obediently into maturity and victory. Some may wonder why God doesn't just do it all at once and be done with it. There remains the issue of free will, but there is also another principle discovered in the conquering of the land of Canaan by Joshua and the children of Israel.

> And the Lord thy God will put out those nations before thee by little and little: thou mayest not consume them at once, lest the beasts of the field increase upon thee. (Deuteronomy 7:22)

We are brought carefully in the timing of the Holy Spirit from *glory to glory*. It will take time for God to work in us that perfect work, but we can confidently say with the apostle Paul, "For I know whom I have believed, and am persuaded that he is able to keep that which I have committed unto him against that day" (2 Timothy 1:12 KJV).

Prayer

Lord, you have promised that you would never leave us or forsake us. As we go through the battles of life, let us sense your presence, your strength, your grace. For it is in you that we live, and move, and have our being. In Jesus's name. Amen.

God Has Left the Building

Hidden back in what the country preacher called *the clean pages* of Scripture is an amazing account of the glory of God manifest in real time, actually moving from place to place. His visible manifestation as a cloud by day and a pillar of fire by night led the children of Israel from Egypt and slavery in the exodus. The vision of Ezekiel, the prophet of the captivity, revealed in the Spirit the invisible supernatural events behind the scenes, beyond what natural man could perceive.

It started like this:

> And it came to pass in the sixth year, in the sixth month, in the fifth day of the month, as I sat in mine house, and the elders of Judah sat before me, that the hand of the Lord God fell there upon me. Then I beheld, and lo a likeness as the appearance of fire: from the appearance of his loins even downward, fire; and from his loins even upward, as the appearance of brightness, as the colour of amber. And he put forth the form of an hand, and took me by a lock of mine head; and the

> spirit lifted me up between the earth and the heaven, and brought me in the visions of God to Jerusalem, to the door of the inner gate that looketh toward the north; where was the seat of the image of jealousy, which provoketh to jealousy. And, behold, the glory of the God of Israel was there, according to the vision that I saw in the plain. (Ezekiel 8:1–4 KJV)

Though the heavens and earth were created ex nihilo, out of nothing, the history of the created world did not take place in a vacuum. This part of the history of the Jewish people, the children of Abraham, took place well after the golden years of King David and King Solomon. The nation had split after the death of Solomon. The Northern Kingdom, Israel, had drifted quickly into idolatry and foolishness under King Jereboam. The whole nation, now called the ten lost tribes of Israel, was eventually destroyed by the Assyrians.

Only a miracle preserved the Southern Kingdom, Judah, but a little more than a century later, they went into captivity under the Babylonian king, Nebuchadnezzar. During this time period, God brought three prophets onto center stage, Daniel in the courts of Babylon, Ezekiel with the ten thousand or so captives relocated and settled in Babylon, and Jeremiah, who remained in a broken Jerusalem with only the poorest people of the land.

From his place with the elders in captivity, Ezekiel found himself caught up in the Spirit and taken to Jerusalem to see for himself the devastation and judgment of a nation that had forgotten God. What he saw there in the Spirit was confirmed by the natural historical events taking place upon the earth.

1. The Image of Jealousy

> Then said he unto me, Son of man, lift up thine eyes now the way toward the north. So I lifted up mine eyes the way toward the north, and behold northward at the gate of the altar this image of jealousy in the entry. He said furthermore unto me, Son of man, seest thou what they do? even the great abominations that the house of Israel committeth here, that I should go far off from my sanctuary? but turn thee yet again, and thou shalt see greater abominations. (Ezekiel 8:5–6 KJV)

When the children of Israel left four hundred years of slavery in Egypt, they were not poor, orphaned, wandering nomads—they had a land promised to their father Abraham. More importantly, they had the visible presence of God. When Moses requested for himself to see the face of God, he was placed in *a cleft of the rock* and protected by the hand of God. Though no man could see God's face, Moses watched as the glory of God passed by him. This experience forever changed him, but there followed a strict injunction.

> Observe thou that which I command thee this day: behold, I drive out before thee the Amorite, and the Canaanite, and the Hittite, and the Perizzite, and the Hivite, and the Jebusite. Take heed to thyself, lest thou make a covenant with the inhabitants of the land whither thou goest, lest it be for a snare in the midst of thee: But ye shall destroy their altars, break their images, and cut down their groves: For thou shalt worship no other god: for the Lord, whose name is Jealous, is a jealous God. (Exodus 34:11–14 KJV)

This followed similar words in the giving of the Ten Commandments, which says:

> Thou shalt have no other gods before me. Thou shalt not make unto thee any graven image, or any likeness of any thing that is in heaven above, or that is in the earth beneath, or that is in the water under the earth: Thou shalt not bow down thyself to them, nor serve them: for I the Lord thy God am a jealous God. (Exodus 20:3–5 KJV)

Isaiah wrote plainly in another time about the foolishness of turning to idols. He tells of a man who builds a fire, cooks his meal, sits down and carves a wooden figure, and then bows down to worship it.

> And none considereth in his heart, neither is there knowledge nor understanding to say, I have burned part of it in the fire; yea, also I have baked bread upon the coals thereof; I have roasted flesh, and eaten it: and shall I make the residue thereof an abomination? shall I fall down to the stock of a tree? He feedeth on ashes: a deceived heart hath turned him aside, that he cannot deliver his soul, nor say, Is there not a lie in my right hand? (Isaiah 44:19–20 KJV)

What an amazing blindness is upon mankind, an astounding confusion of mind! Our wonderful Creator, God, designed the earth to be inhabited, gave life and breath to all, and purposed within himself that he would have children. Jesus himself revealed God as Father, a loving Father, *not willing that any should perish.* For any person to turn from the one, true God to worship anything else is blasphemy and foolishness. It leads to destruction and death. Yet here at the entrance to the north gate was an image, an idol, a false god. There is more.

2. The Elders

> He said furthermore unto me, Son of man, seest thou what they do? even the great abominations that the house of Israel committeth here, that I should go far off from my sanctuary? but turn thee yet again, and thou shalt see greater abominations. And he brought me to the door of the court; and when I looked, behold a hole in the wall. Then said he unto me, Son of man, dig now in the wall: and when I had digged in the wall, behold a door. And he said unto me, Go in, and behold the wicked abominations that they do here. So I went in and saw; and behold every form of creeping things, and abominable beasts, and all the idols of the house of Israel, pourtrayed upon the wall round about. And there stood before them seventy men of the ancients of the house of Israel, and in the midst of them stood Jaazaniah the son of Shaphan, with every man his censer in his hand; and a thick cloud of incense went up. (Ezekiel 8:6–11 KJV)

The elders were the leadership of Israel. It would be expected that the elders, the ancients, would gain wisdom and understanding along with their grey hair.

Instead, they too had turned to idols that included *creeping things and abominable beast.* Ezekiel is not afraid to name names as he mentions in particular, Jaazaniah, the son of Shaphan. This shows again that Ezekiel was indeed able to see natural events from a supernatural perspective. God even gave an explanation to Ezekiel for such ungodly behavior.

> Then said he unto me, Son of man, hast thou seen what the ancients of the house of Israel do in the dark, every man in the chambers of his imagery? for they say, The Lord seeth us not; the Lord hath forsaken the earth. (Ezekiel 8:12 KJV)

Natural and manmade disasters create a dividing point, a pivot point that either turns the heart of man to God or away from God. Like with Job, there are questions that need to be answered in such times. These trials are common to man, no matter that they are national or local in nature. The Scripture indicates these trials are common to man and to a fallen world.

> A person or society that ignores the Creator is ignoring the most important part of reality, and to ignore reality is irrational. (Phillip E. Johnson)

3. The Weeping Women

As though this was not enough, God declares:

> Turn thee yet again, and thou shalt see greater abominations that they do. Then he brought me to the door of the gate of the Lord's house which was toward the north; and, behold, there sat women weeping for Tammuz. (Ezekiel 8:13–14 KJV)

Tammuz was one of a virtual pantheon of gods and a mixture of any number of god-stories. The Syrian story probably in view here was of the death of a beautiful shepherdess killed by a wild boar. The grief caused tears to flow on her behalf to bring her back to life, and this activity became mingled with earth stories of summer and winter and then again to fertility rites. The grief and weeping were often followed by prostitution. As though this was not abomination enough for the women of Israel, there was more and greater to follow.

4. The Young Men

> And he brought me into the inner court of the Lord's house, and, behold, at the door of the temple of the Lord, between the porch and the altar, were about five and twenty men, with their backs toward

> the temple of the Lord, and their faces toward the east; and they worshipped the sun toward the east. (Ezekiel 8:16 KJV)

From the elders to the women to the men, God shows Ezekiel the utter depravity of a nation in the throes of apostasy. The instructions for the tabernacle of Israel had the gate toward the east. The word itself literally carries the idea of the front. Here we find the young men with their backs to the holy place, worshipping the sun. The perversion that looks to the created rather than to the Creator becomes obvious.

> For the invisible things of him from the creation of the world are clearly seen, being understood by the things that are made, even his eternal power and Godhead; so that they are without excuse: Because that, when they knew God, they glorified him not as God, neither were thankful; but became vain in their imaginations, and their foolish heart was darkened. Professing themselves to be wise, they became fools, And changed the glory of the uncorruptible God into an image made like to corruptible man, and to birds, and fourfooted beasts, and creeping things. Wherefore God also gave them up to uncleanness through the lusts of their own hearts, to dishonour their own bod-

> ies between themselves: Who changed the truth of God into a lie, and worshipped and served the creature more than the Creator, who is blessed for ever. Amen. (Romans 1:20–25 KJV)

Judgment

> Then he said unto me, Hast thou seen this, O son of man? Is it a light thing to the house of Judah that they commit the abominations which they commit here? for they have filled the land with violence, and have returned to provoke me to anger: and, lo, they put the branch to their nose. (Ezekiel 8:17 KJV)

Ezekiel had certainly seen what God in his holiness had seen from Israel. There are many notions about the phrase *branch to the nose* but it may have been a colloquialism or a proverb. It appears to be a good translation, but the meaning is obscure, perhaps a lifting of the nose in scorn. Regardless of the background of that particular saying, the provocation to anger was justified.

Destruction and First Movement

> He cried also in mine ears with a loud voice, saying, Cause them that have charge over the city to draw near, even every man

> with his destroying weapon in his hand. And, behold, six men came from the way of the higher gate, which lieth toward the north, and every man a slaughter weapon in his hand; and one man among them was clothed with linen, with a writer's inkhorn by his side: and they went in, and stood beside the brasen altar. And the glory of the God of Israel was gone up from the cherub, whereupon he was, to the threshold of the house. And he called to the man clothed with linen, which had the writer's inkhorn by his side. (Ezekiel:1–3 KJV)

Having made the case for judgment, God calls for the destroyers with weapons for the *breaking in pieces,* literally. The six were armed for the destruction of Jerusalem, but there was one among them in linen and prepared for writing. This writer, or scribe, is assigned to go throughout the city and mark the foreheads of the righteous that they might be spared. In the midst of judgment, there was mercy. Like Abraham centuries before at the destruction of Sodom and Gomorrah.

> That be far from thee to do after this manner, to slay the righteous with the wicked: and that the righteous should be as the wicked, that be far from thee: Shall not the Judge of all the earth do right? (Genesis 18:25 KJV)

The mark is identified only by the Hebrew *taav*, meaning a mark or by implication a signature. It reminds us of the 144,000 belonging to the Lamb, "having his Father's name written in their foreheads" (Revelation 14:1 KJV). That reference takes us back to the man in linen himself, perhaps the Christ preincarnate. Who but the Lord Jesus could so know the hearts and minds of men?

What catches our attention here is the movement of God's glory. It is described here as moving from the cherub, from the mercy seat upon the ark of the covenant. The Holy of Holies in the tabernacle and in the temple had no natural light, no candles, no fire, and no windows. God himself and his glory were the light. To Moses, it appeared as a burning bush that was not consumed. To all of Israel at Mt. Sinai, it was a terrible storm within a dark cloud, but with thunders, lightning, earthquakes, and the sound of many voices and a loud trumpet. It was a pillar of fire by night as they wandered toward the land of Israel. What Ezekiel sees is that very glory, that very manifest presence of God, move from between the golden cherub on the mercy seat to the threshold of the temple.

Second Movement

> Then the glory of the Lord went up from the cherub, and stood over the threshold of the house; and the house was filled with the cloud, and the court was full of the brightness of the Lord's glory. (Ezekiel 10:4 KJV)

As judgment is brought to a close, Ezekiel is permitted to see the throne of God as he had seen at his calling. This description is recorded in the first chapters of the Book of Ezekiel. This is no golden replica, but the very throne of God, high above the firmament. God's glory, having moved from the ark of the covenant to the threshold, now moves above the threshold. The glory of God shines brightly, not hidden behind the veil in the Holy of Holies but filling the temple and the courtyard of the temple with his glory.

Third Movement

> Then the glory of the Lord departed from off the threshold of the house, and stood over the cherubims. And the cherubims lifted up their wings, and mounted up from the earth in my sight: when they went out, the wheels also were beside them, and every one stood at the door of the east gate of the Lord's house; and the glory of the God of Israel was over them above. (Ezekiel 10:18–19 KJV)

Now, the glory of God, the very presence of Almighty God, lifted and mounted the great throne. God had in essence left the building designed and built so that he could dwell in the midst of his people. True to his promise, God brought his people back from the Babylonian captivity after seventy years—but it was never the same again. The restoration prophets, Haggai, Zechariah, and Malachi, all spoke to those of the captivity who returned to Jerusalem. Then there were four hundred years of silence. Not a prophetic voice was heard until that of John the Baptist preparing the way for the Messiah.

Conclusion

> And the Lord God formed man of the dust of the ground, and breathed into his nostrils the breath of life; and man became a living soul. (Genesis 2:7 KJV)

It may seem a simplification to define man as a tri-part being, but from the creation account, we can see that man has a body formed from the dust of the ground. When God breathed life into that body, the result was a living soul. The soul, some say, can be defined as mind, emotion, and will. When God declared that sin would bring death, he spoke truly, man was separated from God spiritually. Death simply means separation. A body may lie in the morgue, but with no animating life (or spirit). There is no resulting expression of the soul. The person is dead.

Jesus told Nicodemus that he needed to be born again. This was an unusual concept for Nicodemus, thinking only in the natural how such a thing could be. Jesus's answer was definitive.

> That which is born of the flesh is flesh; and that which is born of the Spirit is spirit. (John 3:6 KJV)

The Scripture says again that we are "dead in trespasses and sins" (Ephesians 2:1). Very much like the empty temple, we ourselves find ourselves living in only the natural man with a frail body and soul untouched by the living Spirit of God. We move inexorably towards the death of our body, our shell. Just as the Holy of Holies was emptied of the presence of God, the building remains for a while, but the life is gone. However, there is good news.

> And if Christ be in you, the body is dead because of sin; but the Spirit is life because of righteousness. But if the Spirit of him that raised up Jesus from the dead dwell in you, he that raised up Christ from the dead shall also quicken your mortal bodies by his Spirit that dwelleth in you. (Romans 8:10–11 KJV)

> Even when we were dead in sins, hath quickened us together with Christ, (by grace ye are saved). (Ephesians 2:5 KJV)

The apostle Paul, calling himself the chiefest of sinners, understood the great emptiness without Christ. His was a world only of rules, laws, and fleshly ambitions until the living Christ revealed himself to him and changed him forever.

> This is how he explained his experience and new life: "I am crucified with Christ: nevertheless I live; yet not I, but Christ liveth in me: and the life which I now live in the flesh I live by the faith of the Son of God, who loved me, and gave himself for me." (Galatians 2:20 KJV)

Prayer

Father God, you alone give life. Forgive us when we seek it from any other place or in any other thing. Grant to us the authority of your children to reject fear and receive from you the promise of power, love, and a sound mind. In Jesus's name. Amen.

The Cut Covenant

> In the same day the Lord made a covenant with Abram, saying, Unto thy seed have I given this land, from the river of Egypt unto the great river, the river Euphrates.
>
> —Genesis 15:18 KJV

At the beginning of Abraham's pilgrimage, God said to him, "I will show thee" the land (12:1). Later, he said, "I will give it unto thee" (13:15–17). But now, his word is, "To your descendants I have given this land" (15:18, NASB). God's covenant made it a settled matter: The land belongs to Abraham's descendants through Isaac by the Word of God. God's promise to Abraham included basically three things: 1) a son (which we now know to have been Isaac), 2) a land (which we now know to be the land of Israel), and 3) a blessing that would encompass the whole world (which we now understand to be the Messiah, the Christ). This promise was repeated to Abraham at least six times, but here in Genesis 15, we have a unique look into the making of the covenant.

> After these things the word of the Lord came unto Abram in a vision, saying, Fear not, Abram: I am thy shield, and thy exceeding great reward. And Abram said, Lord God, what wilt thou give me, seeing I go childless, and the steward of my house is this Eliezer of Damascus? And Abram said, Behold, to me thou hast given no seed: and, lo, one born in my house is mine heir. And, behold, the word of the Lord came unto him, saying, This shall not be thine heir; but he that shall come forth out of thine own bowels shall be thine heir. And he brought him forth abroad, and said, Look now toward heaven, and tell the stars, if thou be able to number them: and he said unto him, So shall thy seed be. And he believed in the Lord; and he counted it to him for righteousness. (Genesis 15:1–6 KJV)

That God would speak to Abraham so many times is amazing enough, but to see the questions that remained in Abraham's mind is to see the nature of earthbound man. It may be easy enough to say, "God said it! I believe it! That settles it!" but the working out of the utterly fantastic promises of God to his people may not always be understood. The New Testament shares both stories of the angel Gabriel appearing to Mary and Zacharias about the birth of Jesus and of John the Baptist. Both questioned how this amazing thing was to be accomplished, but Mary questioned in faith, while Zacharias was struck mute for not believing. What we know about Abraham is that he believed God, but he could not possibly understand how God would do it. God was gracious to explain it to him and to establish the covenant in a way Abraham would understand.

> And he said unto him, I am the Lord that brought thee out of Ur of the Chaldees, to give thee this land to inherit it. And he said, Lord God, whereby shall I know that I shall inherit it? And he said unto him, Take me an heifer of three years old, and a she goat of three years old, and a ram of three years old, and a turtledove, and a young pigeon. And he took unto him all these, and divided them in the midst, and laid each piece one against another: but the birds divided he not. And when the fowls came down upon the carcases, Abram drove them away. (Genesis 15:7–11 KJV)

Covenants between men or families or nations were common then as now. It could be as simple as a statement of terms, often confirmed by an oath. The modern handshake signaled such an agreement, though at times between known parties it was said, "Their word is good enough for me." It may be understood in a legal sense to place a hand on the Bible and swear, "So help me, God." Even in ancient times, an oath was considered sacred because God watched over it. One example is that of Laban speaking an agreement with Jacob, "See, God is witness betwixt me and thee" (Genesis 31:50).

In some cases, there was even a curse involved as a concluding part of the agreement. On any early American playground you might hear, "Cross my heart and hope to die," not as much as a curse but a proof of sincerity.

In this case, God was performing what was known as the cut covenant. Usually, an animal was killed and its flesh divided and laid out. The principals would come together in the midst of the animal flesh with a general understanding that if either broke their solemn oath, so would they be cut into pieces. Even in the times of the prophet Jeremiah, such oaths were made in a covenant.

> And I will give the men that have transgressed my covenant, which have not performed the words of the covenant which they had made before me, when they cut the calf in twain, and passed between the parts thereof, The princes of Judah, and the princes of Jerusalem, the eunuchs, and the priests, and all the people of the land, which passed between the parts of the calf; I will even give them into the hand of their enemies, and into the hand of them that seek their life: and their dead bodies shall be for meat unto the fowls of the heaven,

> and to the beasts of the earth. (Jeremiah 34:18–20 KJV)

In this account, though, there are some striking differences. Having divided the living animals and birds as God had directed, Abraham worked diligently to keep the vultures off them.

> And when the sun was going down, a deep sleep fell upon Abram; and, lo, an horror of great darkness fell upon him. (Genesis 15:12 KJV)

From out of this great darkness, God repeated his promises to Abraham. Abraham was made to understand that though he would die and be *buried in a good old age*, the promises would continue through his descendants.

> And it came to pass, that, when the sun went down, and it was dark, behold a smoking furnace, and a burning lamp that passed between those pieces. In the same day the Lord made a covenant with Abram, saying, Unto thy seed have I given this land, from the river of Egypt unto the great river, the river Euphrates. (Genesis 15:17 KJV)

The smoking furnace and burning lamp passed between the pieces of sacrificial flesh, much like a person would do in the human act of the cut covenant. Here, however, Abraham is outside of the action. God had revealed his plan to Abraham in previous communications (Gen 12, 13), but here, the covenant is made with Abraham. Though this covenant is made with Abraham, it is not a contract between two equal parties with mutual obligations. Rather, God himself is establishing the covenant as a disposition, as an act of grace that Abraham receives by faith.

> And this I say, that the covenant, that was confirmed before of God in Christ, the law, which was four hundred and thirty years after, cannot disannul, that it should make the promise of none effect. For if the inheritance be of the law, it is no more of promise: but God gave it to Abraham by promise. (Galatians 3:17–18)

We are constantly reminded in Scripture that trust in God and faith in God is the key. And that even the faith itself is a gift of God, a response to the revelation of his grace and mercy.

> For by grace are ye saved through faith; and that not of yourselves: it is the gift of God: Not of works, lest any man should boast. (Ephesians 2:8–9 KJV)

We are indeed the *sheep of his pasture,* but it is the Great Shepherd himself that leads us beside still waters, that restores our souls, and that brings us into green pastures. It is from our wonderful Heavenly Father that *all blessings flow.* Faith is a wonderful and beautiful thing, but the glory of faith is the object of our faith. We are so much like the man who brought his demon-possessed son to Jesus:

> Jesus said unto him, If thou canst believe, all things are possible to him that believeth. And straightway the father of the child cried out, and said with tears, Lord, I believe; help thou mine unbelief. (Mark 9:23–24 KJV)

The promise is given by a faithful Heavenly Father. What remains? That we believe him. It is at this point that the writer of Hebrews reminds us, "For when God made promise to Abraham, because he could swear by no greater, he sware by himself, Saying, Surely blessing I will bless thee, and multiplying I will multiply thee" (Hebrews 6:13–14).

The explanation for this extraordinary event follows.

> For men verily swear by the greater: and an oath for confirmation is to them an end of all strife. Wherein God, willing more abundantly to shew unto the heirs of promise the immutability of his counsel, confirmed it by an oath: That by two immutable things, in which it was impossible for God to lie, we might have a strong consolation, who have fled for ref-

> uge to lay hold upon the hope set before us. (Hebrews 6:16–18 KJV)

Because God could swear by no greater than himself, so he did. There are two things here that speak volumes about his faithfulness. First, that God was willing to show to the heirs of promise his immutable, unchangeable counsel. This counsel was decided before the foundation of the world.

> According as he hath chosen us in him before the foundation of the world, that we should be holy and without blame before him in love: Having predestinated us unto the adoption of children by Jesus Christ to himself, according to the good pleasure of his will, To the praise of the glory of his grace, wherein he hath made us accepted in the beloved. (Ephesians 1:4–6 KJV)

This was and is God's plan. The One who sees the end from the beginning, the One who is the Alpha and the Omega, the beginning and the end—he is also the Author and the Finisher of our faith. Being omniscient, the entire Scriptures reveal God's love and purpose for man from Genesis to Revelation.

Then secondly, that God was willing to confirm it by an oath to Abraham in a manner that Abraham would understand. And not just Abraham, but all who would follow him in believing the promises of God.

> Know ye therefore that they which are of faith, the same are the children of Abraham. And the scripture, foreseeing that God would justify the heathen through faith, preached before the gospel unto Abraham, saying, In thee shall all nations be blessed. (Galatians 3:7–8 KJV)

What then shall we say to these things?

> O the depth of the riches both of the wisdom and knowledge of God! how unsearchable are his judgments, and his ways past finding out! For who hath known the mind of the Lord? or who hath been his counsellor? Or who hath first given to him, and it shall be recompensed unto him again? For of him, and through him, and to him, are all things: to whom be glory for ever. Amen. (Romans 11:33–36 KJV)

Prayer

Gracious Father, how often we forget how determined you are to be Father to your children! You have determined an inheritance for us that eye has not seen, that ear has not heard, that the mind of a man could not possibly comprehend! O Father, remind us again of your great love that you are so determined to reveal to us by your Spirit!

God in a Box

And the word of Samuel came to all Israel.

—1 Samuel 4:1–5

Before there were kings in Israel, there were judges. These judges were raised up by God at particular times in Israel's history when the nation was threatened. Before there were judges, there were priests and the Levitical priesthood. Before there were priests in Israel, there were fathers like Job and Abraham that led their families to a knowledge of the One True God by prayer and sacrifices.

Eli was descended from Ithamar, the fourth son of Aaron, the first high priest, and brother of Moses. Eli was the first to combine the office of judge and high priest in Israel (1 Samuel 4:18) and served as a judge in Israel for forty years. The passage of office from father to son was a common mechanism in the life of Israel's leadership. God's choice of the Levites as priests had established precedent, but it had not worked out as well for the office of judges.

Eli's sons, Hophni and Phineas, were a disappointment to their father and to the Israelites who came to worship at Shiloh. The very presence of the ark of the covenant and the tabernacle had made Shiloh the center of worship. The

Scripture records: "Now the sons of Eli were sons of Belial; they knew not the Lord" (1 Samuel 2:12 KJV).

Taking meat offerings by force from worshippers was one thing, but they also took women of their choosing right in front of the tabernacle. Nothing Eli said could dissuade them from their evil ways.

> Wherefore the sin of the young men was very great before the Lord: for men abhorred the offering of the Lord. (1 Samuel 2:17 KJV)

A nameless prophet had confronted Eli with the profligacy of his sons and predicted that both would die at the same time. His family lineage would not continue as priests and his descendants would not have long and productive lives.

> Wherefore the Lord God of Israel saith, I said indeed that thy house, and the house of thy father, should walk before me for ever: but now the Lord saith, Be it far from me; for them that honour me I will honour, and they that despise me shall be lightly esteemed. Behold, the days come, that I will cut off thine arm, and the arm of thy father's house, that there shall not be an old man in thine house. (1 Samuel 2:30–31 KJV)

It was in this setting that Samuel came to minister before Eli and before the Lord. Though Samuel came from Levitical lineage, not all Levites were priests and there was certainly no precedent for him to become a judge in Israel. Few Scriptural accounts are as popular with children as the story of Samuel first hearing the Word of the Lord. However, many children and adults are unaware of what God spoke to him. Eli had to press him earnestly the next day to tell him exactly what the Lord had said. Under this duress, Samuel repeated the Lord's condemnation upon the family of Eli. It seems a heavy load for so young a child. The Scripture records that all of Israel became aware that Samuel was called to be a prophet.

> And Samuel grew, and the Lord was with him, and did let none of his words fall to the ground. And all Israel from Dan even to Beer-sheba knew that Samuel was established to be a prophet of the Lord. (1 Samuel 3:19–20 KJV)

The fulfillment of the prophecy was not long in coming.

> Now Israel went out against the Philistines to battle, and pitched beside Eben-ezer: and the Philistines pitched in Aphek. And the Philistines put themselves in array against Israel: and when they joined battle, Israel was smitten before the Philistines:

> and they slew of the army in the field about four thousand men. (1 Samuel 4:1–2 KJV)

The Philistines were the descendants of Ham that inhabited the plains of southwest Palestine along the shores of the Great Sea, the Mediterranean. Their cities were unchallenged by the Israelites as they came into the promised land under Joshua and they became a thorn and testing to the children of Israel later. This unexpected defeat at the hands of their enemy was devastating to Israel since they fully expected the God of Israel to miraculously defend them as in the past.

> And when the people were come into the camp, the elders of Israel said, Wherefore hath the Lord smitten us to day before the Philistines? Let us fetch the ark of the covenant of the Lord out of Shiloh unto us, that, when it cometh among us, it may save us out of the hand of our enemies. So the people sent to Shiloh, that they might bring from thence the ark of the covenant of the Lord of hosts, which dwelleth between the cherubims: and the two sons of Eli, Hophni and Phinehas, were there with the ark of the covenant of God. And when the ark of the covenant of the Lord came into the camp, all Israel shouted

> with a great shout, so that the earth rang again. (1 Samuel 4:3–5 KJV)

In just these few verses, the power and presumption of religion are revealed. Though they asked the right question, "Why are we smitten?" They seem unmoved to search for an answer. Instead, they decide to bring the ark of the covenant to the battle site. Their reasoning seems to be *that it may save us*. Rather than a humble supplication to the One True God of all heaven and earth, they resort to what may be seen of him, that is, his manifest place in the Holy of Holies upon the mercy seat. Hophni and Phineas have already been described as blatant hypocrites, not knowing nor serving the God of Israel except in their priestly position only. They fully intend to manipulate God and their religion to gain the upper hand.

Later, at another time, the prophet Jeremiah warned Israel of this very tendency to see the visible signs of God, the ark and the temple, instead of worshipping God *in spirit and in truth* as Jesus would later declare.

> Trust ye not in lying words, saying, The temple of the Lord, The temple of the Lord, The temple of the Lord, are these. For if ye throughly amend your ways and your doings; if ye throughly execute judgment between a man and his neighbour; If ye oppress not the stranger, the fatherless, and the widow, and shed not innocent blood in this place, neither walk

> after other gods to your hurt: Then will I cause you to dwell in this place, in the land that I gave to your fathers, for ever and ever. Behold, ye trust in lying words, that cannot profit. Will ye steal, murder, and commit adultery, and swear falsely, and burn incense unto Baal, and walk after other gods whom ye know not; And come and stand before me in this house, which is called by my name, and say, We are delivered to do all these abominations? Is this house, which is called by my name, become a den of robbers in your eyes? Behold, even I have seen it, saith the Lord. (Jeremiah 7:4–11 KJV)

Despite the encouragement created by the coming of the ark into the battlefield, this crass manipulation of the ark and God's presence did not succeed. Even the Philistines were swayed by this deception and expected to be totally defeated by the God of Israel, but instead were victorious over Israel and captured the ark.

The idea that God is a local god comes up again and again in the history of the world and in religions all over the world. It is instructive to see how God responded to this when Syria moved against Israel years later.

> And there came a man of God, and spake unto the king of Israel, and said, Thus saith the Lord, Because the Syrians have

> said, The Lord is God of the hills, but he is not God of the valleys, therefore will I deliver all this great multitude into thine hand, and ye shall know that I am the Lord. (1 Kings 20:28 KJV)

Thinking that their local god, Dagon, had defeated another local god, the Philistines placed the ark in the temple of Dagon. After all, if one god is good, then two must be twice as good. The more gods the better. Like the Athenians on Mars Hill, superstition added to superstition is like building on sand. Their victory seemed complete, but it was short-lived.

> And the Philistines took the ark of God, and brought it from Eben-ezer unto Ashdod. When the Philistines took the ark of God, they brought it into the house of Dagon, and set it by Dagon. And when they of Ashdod arose early on the morrow, behold, Dagon was fallen upon his face to the earth before the ark of the Lord. And they took Dagon, and set him in his place again. (1 Samuel 5:1–3 KJV)

Though the ark of God was not in its place in Israel, the God of the ark was still God over all the earth. Dagon could not stand before him. Dagon appears to be the *fish god*, the top half being the form of a man and the lower being a fish. Replacing him to his pedestal and reinforcing him with nails did little to bolster the confidence of the Dagon priesthood. Serving false gods brings only superstition and servitude. It is one wrong step that multiplies into a thousand lies, repeating generational curses passed down from parent to child again and again. It establishes habits of thinking unbroken by common sense and truth.

> Hear, O Israel: The Lord our God is one Lord: And thou shalt love the Lord thy God with all thine heart, and with all thy soul, and with all thy might. (Deuteronomy 6:4–5 KJV)

The New Testament declares:

> For there is one God, and one mediator between God and men, the man Christ Jesus; Who gave himself a ransom for all, to be testified in due time. (1 Timothy 2:5–6 KJV)

Isaiah details graphically how a man builds a fire, cooks his food, and then carves out a god for himself from the wood left over from burning.

> They have not known nor understood: for he hath shut their eyes, that they cannot see; and their hearts, that they cannot understand. And none considereth in his heart, neither is there knowledge nor understanding to say, I have burned part

> of it in the fire; yea, also I have baked bread upon the coals thereof; I have roasted flesh, and eaten it: and shall I make the residue thereof an abomination? shall I fall down to the stock of a tree? He feedeth on ashes: a deceived heart hath turned him aside, that he cannot deliver his soul, nor say, Is there not a lie in my right hand? (Isaiah 44:18–20 KJV)

Plagues began to appear in the people of Ashdod and surrounding cities, tumors in their private parts, and an outbreak of mice. The Scripture declares that *the hand of the Lord was heavy upon them of Ashdod.* Moving the ark of the covenant to other cities did not help. First Ashdod, then Gath, and then Ekron. The people of Ekron caught on quickly to what was happening.

> And it came to pass, as the ark of God came to Ekron, that the Ekronites cried out, saying, They have brought about the ark of the God of Israel to us, to slay us and our people. (1 Samuel 5:10 KJV)

The ark was in Philistia for seven months and those not killed by the plague were dealing with tumors. Finally, they called for diviners and priests for wisdom to end it all and to send the ark back to Israel. They began to remember the plagues upon Pharaoh and Egypt, leading up to the exodus. They were over their heads with the God of Israel and they knew it. Preparing an offering of gold images of both mice and tumors, they placed the ark on a cart pulled by two cows separated from their calves. If the cows moved on down the road toward Israel and did not return to their calves, then they would know it was really from God. The Scripture records that the cows did not turn to the left or right but headed to Israel. The Philistines followed the cows and cart all the way to the border, made sure it was received by the Israelites, and then returned home.

It would be easy to think that this is the happy ending to the story. What happened next reveals once again that the God of Israel is not a local god, but the One True God. The God of the whole earth.

> And he smote the men of Beth-shemesh, because they had looked into the ark of the Lord, even he smote of the people fifty thousand and threescore and ten men: and the people lamented, because the Lord had smitten many of the people with a great slaughter. And the men of Beth-shemesh said, Who is able to stand before this holy Lord God? and to whom shall he go up from us? (1 Samuel 6:19–20 KJV)

Their joy at the return of the ark to Israel must have been tempered by the fact that the ark had been in enemy hands for seven months. Inside the ark, beneath the solid gold mercy seat, were artifacts of particular significance to all Israel, the tablets of the Ten Commandments, Aaron's rod that budded, and a pot of manna supernaturally kept fresh.

The men of Beth-shemesh must have wondered if the Philistines had taken those precious items from the ark. Forgetting, or ignoring, all the priestly protocols established by God so that his presence could remain with his people, they removed the mercy seat.

The results were disastrous. There is some question concerning the exact number of men killed as the holy presence of God broke out upon them, but that there was a great slaughter is beyond doubt. The question that arose immediately from their lips was, "Who is able to stand before this holy Lord God?" It reminds us again of Uzzah.

> And when they came to Nachon's threshingfloor, Uzzah put forth his hand to the ark of God, and took hold of it; for the oxen shook it. And the anger of the Lord was kindled against Uzzah; and God smote him there for his error; and there he died by the ark of God. (2 Samuel 6:6–7 KJV)

As C. S. Lewis described Aslan in his famous Chronicles of Narnia, "he is not a tame lion."

> But who may abide the day of his coming? and who shall stand when he appeareth? for he is like a refiner's fire. (Malachi 3:2 KJV)

> If thou, Lord, shouldest mark iniquities, O Lord, who shall stand? But there is forgiveness with thee, that thou mayest be feared. (Psalm 130:3–4 KJV)

Prayer

Holy Father, you seem so far away and unapproachable from our earthly view. Yet, you are not far from any one of us—not just with us, but also in us! What grace and mercy you have shown your oft rebellious children! Father, we thank you that you have brought us back to you through our Lord Jesus Christ.

We Ought to Obey God

> Let every soul be subject unto the higher powers. For there is no power but of God: the powers that be are ordained of God.
>
> —Romans 13:1

> To the intent that the living may know that the most High ruleth in the kingdom of men, and giveth it to whomsoever he will, and setteth up over it the basest of men.
>
> —Daniel 4:17 KJV

There is a reason behind the old adage about barbers avoiding conversations about religion and politics. As the popular sayings go, may be one of the best known but least applied. Another popular saying about death and taxes reveals that both religion and politics are universal experiences. These life experiences are common to man. Because they involve the concept of authority, the responses are often quite passionate. Regardless of the various translations of Romans 13, all scripture reveals that

God is the source of all authority and all earthly authority is a derived authority. Another popular translation reads, "Everyone must submit himself to the governing authorities, for there is no authority except that which God has established. The authorities that exist have been established by God" (Romans 13:1–2 NIV).

So, which form of government is best? Someone has said, "Democracy is the worst form of government, except for all the rest." Under English rule in the Middle East, the English generals lamented publicly that they could get nothing done because the various Arab clans would meet for days and weeks to hammer out a solution that involved them all. That was an interesting experiment in democracy. Perhaps a *beneficent dictator* that could make decisions quickly could be the answer.

After the bloodbath of the French Revolution, the American colonies worked feverishly to establish a republic instead of a democracy, often called "mobocracy" or rule by the mob. Then there are those calling for a *theocracy*, the rule by God. The problem there is, of course, the question of who it is that really understands what God wants! What seems apparent is that our gracious God has allowed the free moral agency of mankind to establish government as they please, if only they would live by it and recognize his kingdom as ultimate. Perhaps there is depth to the saying, "People get the government they deserve." It should be that the best government is the one God has established or allows to be established. However, it can change! Daniel found himself in high politics and often encountered divine intervention in government.

> Then was the secret revealed unto Daniel in a night vision. Then Daniel blessed the God of heaven. Daniel answered and said, Blessed be the name of God for ever and ever: for wisdom and might are his: And he changeth the times and the seasons: he removeth kings, and setteth up kings: he giveth wisdom unto the wise, and knowledge to them that know understanding: He revealeth the deep and secret things: he knoweth what is in the darkness, and the light dwelleth with him. (Daniel 2:19–22 KJV)

Though many believe that a Creator God gave the world a spin and disappeared, Daniel reminds us that *the most High ruleth in the kingdom of men.* Not only is the high authority established by God, but the incumbents, the existing authorities, are there by his will as well.

> There is no authority but by act of God, and the existing authorities are instituted by him. (Romans 13:1b NEB)

The apostle Peter repeated this injunction.

> Submit yourselves to every ordinance of man for the Lord's sake: whether it be to the king, as supreme; Or unto governors, as unto them that are sent by him

> for the punishment of evildoers, and for the praise of them that do well. For so is the will of God, that with well doing ye may put to silence the ignorance of foolish men: As free, and not using your liberty for a cloke of maliciousness, but as the servants of God. (1 Peter 2:13–16 KJV)

Paul exhorts prayers for all these in authority and explains further why this is important.

> I exhort therefore, that, first of all, supplications, prayers, intercessions, and giving of thanks, be made for all men; For kings, and for all that are in authority; that we may lead a quiet and peaceable life in all godliness and honesty. (1 Timothy 2:1–2 KJV)

A quiet and peaceable life results as God's will is established in the natural world. As a result of a fallen world, quietness and peace would not be normal. Instead, as man denies God and pulls away from his rule, all the fallen qualities of sin and flesh are unleashed.

The corollary to the fact that God institutes government is plain as well.

> Consequently, he who rebels against the authority is rebelling against what God has instituted, and those who do so will

> bring judgment on themselves. (Romans 13:2 NIV)

National authorities rightly protect themselves from riot, anarchy, and lawlessness. These are legitimate functions of government and those who rebel rightly bring the terror of government upon their heads.

> For rulers are not a terror to good works, but to the evil. Wilt thou then not be afraid of the power? do that which is good, and thou shalt have praise of the same: For he is the minister of God to thee for good. But if thou do that which is evil, be afraid; for he beareth not the sword in vain: for he is the minister of God, a revenger to execute wrath upon him that doeth evil. (Romans 13:3–4 KJV)

The Constitution of the United States calls for the government *to provide for the common defense, and insure domestic tranquility*. It is common to see the words *To Serve and Protect* on police and sheriff vehicles. This is a legitimate and derived authority in the natural arena. Christians, then, obey the law in recognition of God's absolute authority.

> Tell us therefore, What thinkest thou? Is it lawful to give tribute unto Caesar, or not? But Jesus perceived their wickedness, and said, Why tempt ye me, ye

> hypocrites? Shew me the tribute money. And they brought unto him a penny. And he saith unto them, Whose is this image and superscription? They say unto him, Caesar's. Then saith he unto them, Render therefore unto Caesar the things which are Caesar's; and unto God the things that are God's. When they had heard these words, they marvelled, and left him, and went their way. (Matthew 22:17–22 KJV)

The government is given two powers to accomplish its purposes. The first is raw power.

> But if thou do that which is evil, be afraid; for he beareth not the sword in vain: for he is the minister of God, a revenger to execute wrath upon him that doeth evil.

There are always issues to be resolved. There are real differences of opinion concerning capital punishment, excessive force, and all kinds of abuse of power. For instance, the Supreme Court of the United States ruled in 1990 that police checkpoints on New Year's Eve were legal, but that the rights of citizens to not participate was also a legal right. The second power granted to governments is taxation.

> For this cause pay ye tribute also.

Again, the biblical principle is to give to Caesar what is his, but to God what is his.

Three times in these verses, Paul uses the phrase *minister(s) of God* in defining government officials, presented here in order and context from the KJV (King James Version).

> Do that which is good, and thou shalt have praise of the same: For he is the minister of God to thee for good. (Romans 13:3–4)

> But if thou do that which is evil, be afraid; For he beareth not the sword in vain: for he is the minister of God, a revenger to execute wrath upon him that doeth evil. (Romans 13:4)

> For this cause pay ye tribute also: for they are God's ministers, attending continually upon this very thing. (Romans 13:6)

The first two times Paul uses the word for *deacon*, describing the official as an attendant or the waiter at a table or other menial duties. (Much of our American church polity has forgotten this Scriptural definition and become "deacon possessed" as men and women who should be serving become instead dictatorial.)

The third use of the word in Romans 13:6 is decidedly different. It is the Greek word for *priests* whose job is ministering *liturgy,* or in other words, a public servant or functionary. This accords with the founding fathers' understanding of public service as the *consent of the governed* as opposed to rule by royal decree or even dictates of the elite. Even George Washington refused high-sounding titles like *Your Eminence* and instead preferred the simple *Mr. President* still being used today. The functions of these public servants, then, had to do with basic services—mail, roads, utilities, schools, and *thus to provide for the common defense and insure domestic tranquility.*

What happens when the existing powers that be fail to live up to this standard?

> Righteousness exalteth a nation: but sin is a reproach to any people. (Proverbs 14:34 KJV)

> Woe to thee, O land, when thy king is a child, and thy princes eat in the morning! Blessed art thou, O land, when thy king is the son of nobles, and thy princes eat in due season, for strength, and not for drunkenness! (Ecclesiastes 10:16–17 KJV)

The words of Solomon are in a poetic setting, but the meaning is clear. When the rulers or government of a nation or people have no wisdom but are childish and selfish in their desires, even irrational, the people suffer. *Eating in the morning* refers to all the elements of self-indulgence with no regard for a *due season* and for strength. This natural proclivity of fallen man for self-indulgence is conveyed accurately in the saying that power corrupts and absolute power corrupts absolutely.

Phillip E. Johnson famously declared, "A person or a society that ignores the Creator is ignoring the most important part of reality, and to ignore reality is to be irrational."

In a world of explicit examples both historical and anecdotal, we can choose from a plethora of accounts in the Scripture. For example, following the outpouring of the Holy Spirit recorded in Acts 2, the resulting new church found itself opposed by the existing religious authorities.

> Saying, Did not we straitly command you that ye should not teach in this name? and, behold, ye have filled Jerusalem with your doctrine, and intend to bring this man's blood upon us. Then Peter and the other apostles answered and said, We ought to obey God rather than men. (Acts 5:28–29 KJV)

This is not the first example by far of the recognition of God's authority beyond earthly authority. Another example from the Old Testament:

> And the king of Egypt spake to the Hebrew midwives, of which the name of the one was Shiphrah, and the name of the other Puah: And he said, When ye do the office of a midwife to the Hebrew women, and see them upon the stools; if

> it be a son, then ye shall kill him: but if it be a daughter, then she shall live. But the midwives feared God, and did not as the king of Egypt commanded them, but saved the men children alive. (Exodus 1:15–17 KJV)

There is another similar incident in the famous account of Daniel in the lion's den. The Scripture reads, "Then said these men, We shall not find any occasion against this Daniel, except we find it against him concerning the law of his God."

These men conspired to establish a law, though temporary, that prayer should not be offered to any god but only to the king. Daniel, of course, did what he always did.

> Now when Daniel knew that the writing was signed, he went into his house; and his windows being open in his chamber toward Jerusalem, he kneeled upon his knees three times a day, and prayed, and gave thanks before his God, as he did aforetime. Then these men assembled, and found Daniel praying and making supplication before his God. (Daniel 6:10–11 KJV)

This principle of obedience to God before other allegiances became known as the doctrine of the lesser magistrates from the Magdeburg Confession. As the Reformation grew in power and influence from *The Ninety-Five Theses* of Martin Luther, the powers of Emperor Charles V and Pope Paul III merged against the *Protestants*. This was not just a war of words, but lives were at stake. Two years after the death of Martin Luther in 1546, the German people fell under the Augsburg Interim, which demanded a return to catholic practices, including papal abuses, and a renunciation of justification by faith.

By 1550, many pastors and other notable Lutherans had fled to Magdeburg, Germany, with its walls and a more hospitable theology. They became what may have been the last stronghold of Protestantism. Declaring themselves to want only what was already provided to Jews and Muslims, that is, freedom of religion, they would in fact be the very best of citizens because of the requirements of Romans 13. Those requirements, however, could not be used to force Christians to sin against God.

At the very core of the Confession was the doctrine of the lesser magistrates.

> We shall prove that the preservation of this doctrine is necessary for a godly magistrate, and that the dissent of a godly magistrate is just, even against a superior one who is using arms to force the rightly instituted churches of Christ to defect from the acknowledged truth and turn to idolatry.

The point of the confession is exactly that of the disciples: *We ought to obey God rather than men.* Those who signed the Magdeburg Confession understood that some may use the Confession to take up arms against rightful rulers. It was quite possible as well for some to abuse the Confession to defend personal prejudice under the auspices of Scripture. Our modern crisis in the middle of so-called *culture wars* has brought accusations of racism and judgmental condemnation against some very humble and sincere Christians who simply want to do what the Scriptures enjoin—to love God and love our neighbor. The refusal to promote sin, however, is one of the basic premises of religious rights.

In conclusion, God's people, hopefully in word and in deed, will follow the scriptural injunction from Romans 13:5 and 7.

> Wherefore ye must needs be subject, not only for wrath, but also for conscience sake.
>
> Render therefore to all their dues: tribute to whom tribute is due; custom to whom custom; fear to whom fear; honour to whom honour.

This is part and parcel of the admonition in Romans 12:1–3, which declares:

> I beseech you therefore, brethren, by the mercies of God, that ye present your

> bodies a living sacrifice, holy, acceptable unto God, which is your reasonable service. And be not conformed to this world: but be ye transformed by the renewing of your mind, that ye may prove what is that good, and acceptable, and perfect, will of God. For I say, through the grace given unto me, to every man that is among you, not to think of himself more highly than he ought to think; but to think soberly, according as God hath dealt to every man the measure of faith. (KJV)

Prayer

Lord, we get so caught up in the human machinations of our governments. Their faults and failures, their ambitions, all remind us again that they are fallen creatures as well. Help us, Lord, to remember the admonition to pray for them that the land might have peace. In Jesus's name. Amen.

The Names of the King

And I saw heaven opened, and behold a white horse; and he that sat upon him was called Faithful and True, and in righteousness he doth judge and make war.

—Revelation 19:11

Everything seems so natural. Day follows night, weekend follows workweek. But even that simple observation raises questions of origins. For instance, why seven days in a week? At most, everyone understands that a year marks the earth's annual trip around the sun, right at 365.24 days (with an extra day added every four years for our calendar). We can be even more exact concerning the month, following the waxing and waning of the moon in its orbit at 30.436875 days.

With the modern advent of lasers, we can even tell how much the moon is moving away from the earth in its orbit, roughly 3.78 cm per year or about as much as your fingernails grow in a year. (This inconvenient fact destroys most modern *guesstimates* of the age of our solar system, and lunar scientist Irwin Shapiro used to joke, "The best explanation was observational error—the moon does not exist." And yet, there it is.) The fact is our concept of a week of seven days comes from the account of the creation week in Genesis, and of course, the commandment concerning the Sabbath in the Ten Commandments.

As difficult as the origin theories of our universe are in what is called historical science, most scientists are more certain of its ending. Losing all energy and motion, our universe will simply die a heat death. The suns will have gone out, every molecule reduced to zero moving electrons. But not to worry! That will not take place for billions of years.

In our Bibles, we have a remarkable collection of histories and events. They begin in Genesis with the creation of the universe by a wonderful Heavenly Father of limitless power, wisdom, and presence—he is omnipotent, omniscient, and omnipresent. The historical account tells also of the spiritual fall of man and the resulting consequences for the world and everyone and everything in the world. It predicts a Savior who will return the hearts of many to the Father. Following this wonderful account brings us to the Book of Revelation and the actual ending of the world we know now. Once again, it is the Savior, the One risen from the dead that unites again all the beloved children to the Father. It is this Savior, the Lord Jesus Christ, who appears on a white horse and is identified by four different names. A description of who he is and what he does is linked to each name in the text.

1) *I saw heaven standing open and there before me was a white horse, whose rider is called faithful and true. With justice, he judges and makes war.*

In Ray Stedman's article *10 Propositions Concerning War*, he makes the point that war is inevitable in a fallen world and that peace is the exception—it is a gift of God.

> From whence come wars and fightings among you? come they not hence, even of your lusts that war in your members? (James 4:1 KJV)

In an imperfect and fallen world, the concept of justice gets a little fuzzy, especially in warfare. If you read or watch any local, national, or world news at all, it doesn't take long to see man's inhumanity to man and the truth of the apostle James's quote above. It seems that the best we can do is react to an injustice already accomplished. When seconds count, the police are minutes away. Bringing the guilty to punishment is certainly necessary and part of the purpose of government, but it will not bring back the dead, heal the wounds, or rebuild after the arson.

There are just causes for the correction of evil and the punishment of evildoers (Romans 13). For instance, Abraham Lincoln felt that the Civil war was a judgment upon both the North and the South. The South for the evil of slavery and the North for its materialism and godlessness. However, we all *see through a glass darkly,* so to speak, and *we know in part.* We are never able to see the whole picture of perfect justice. It is not so with Christ. It is in his capacity as faithful and true that the rider comes *to judge and to make war.* Because he is faithful and true, he makes a perfect judgment in all things.

> Now when he was in Jerusalem at the passover, in the feast day, many believed in his name, when they saw the miracles which he did. But Jesus did not commit himself unto them, because he knew all men, And needed not that any should testify of man: for he knew what was in man. (John 2:23–25 KJV)

Because he is faithful and true, he brings perfect justice in judging and making war against all injustice and ungodliness. At long last, all of the wrongs and injustices will be avenged and made right.

2) *His eyes are like blazing fire, and on his head are many crowns [diadems]. He has a name written on him that no one but he himself knows.*

His unknown name is linked to the blazing eyes and the many diadems on his head. One of our early American preachers declared, "If a worm can know a man, than a man can know God." Each glimpse we have of Almighty God is more than we can take in as human beings. Moses was not allowed to see the face of God but rather saw his glory from behind. Even then, the hand of God protected him in the cleft of the rock. Because he is God, theologians describe him as *wholly other.* The *blazing eyes* speak of full discernment; his omniscience and penetrating knowledge. *Many diadems* speak of absolute and full authority. Here are omniscience and omnipotence both vested in a human being.

> In the beginning was the Word, and the Word was with God, and the Word was God. The same was in the beginning with God. (John 1:1–2)
>
> And the Word was made flesh, and dwelt among us, (and we beheld his glory, the glory as of the only begotten of the Father,) full of grace and truth. (KJV)

His name, his unknown name, reveals the wonder of Jesus in that as man, he manifests all the fullness of God. He is both God and man.

> God, who at sundry times and in divers manners spake in time past unto the fathers by the prophets, Hath in these last days spoken unto us by his Son, whom he hath appointed heir of all things, by whom also he made the worlds; Who being the brightness of his glory, and the express image of his person, and upholding all things by the word of his power, when he had by himself purged our sins, sat down on the right hand of the Majesty on high. (Hebrews 1:1–3 KJV)

No one knows the full extent of that mysterious union of God and man. In man, Jesus is the full authority, power, omniscience, and omnipotence of God. It is something that no one fully knows or understands.

> And without controversy great is the mystery of godliness: God was manifest in the flesh, justified in the Spirit, seen of angels, preached unto the Gentiles, believed on in the world, received up into glory. (1 Timothy 3:16 KJV)

3) *He is dressed in a robe dipped in blood, and his name is the Word of God. The armies of heaven were following him, riding on white horses and dressed in fine linen, white and clean. Out of his mouth comes a sharp sword with which to strike down the nations.*

The great rider is also called the Word of God. This name is associated with the robe dipped in blood and with the armies of heaven following him, as well as with the sharp sword that comes out of his mouth. There is a somewhat similar account of a warrior-messiah in Isaiah 63. As though the prophet is standing in Jerusalem looking toward the south, toward Edom, he sees a great warrior coming with garments stained red. He asks him a question.

> Who is this that cometh from Edom, with dyed garments from Bozrah? this that is glorious in his apparel, travelling in the greatness of his strength? (Isaiah 63:1–4)

The strong warrior responds and says, "I that speak in righteousness, mighty to save."

Another question, asking, "Wherefore art thou red in thine apparel, and thy garments like him that treadeth in the winefat?"

Another answer—saying,

> I have trodden the winepress alone; and of the people there was none with me: for I will tread them in mine anger, and trample them in my fury; and their blood shall be sprinkled upon my garments, and I will stain all my raiment. For the day of vengeance is in mine heart, and the year of my redeemed is come. (KJV)

There are two quick observations here that remind us of the Lord Jesus Christ, the very Word of God. First, there was no other human being to help the warrior-messiah in judgment. There was not a person on earth without sin who could stand for mankind. Job longed for such a person, a daysman, or mediator, to stand for him.

> For he is not a man, as I am, that I should answer him, and we should come together in judgment. Neither is there any daysman betwixt us, that might lay his hand upon us both. (Job 9:32–33 KJV)

Secondly, in the same breath, the warrior-messiah speaks of judgment, the day of vengeance against all injustice, wickedness, sin, and the year of redemption for his redeemed. The redemption of God's people from a world groaning in sin and hate will be of necessity a division from it and a judgment of it.

The sharp sword, which the prophet sees here in the mouth of Jesus, as in the opening vision (Revelation 1) is the Word of God. It is a symbol, of course, of the power of the Word.

> For the word of God is quick, and powerful, and sharper than any twoedged sword, piercing even to the dividing asunder of soul and spirit, and of the joints and marrow, and is a discerner of the thoughts and intents of the heart. Neither is there any creature that is not manifest in his sight: but all things are naked and opened unto the eyes of him with whom we have to do. (Hebrews 4:12–13 KJV)

Here is portrayed not only the perfect discernment of the Word but the power to judge the nations in perfect discernment. It is, after all, a sword. On the day of Pentecost, the Jews who were listening to Peter's great message, at the end "were cut to the heart" (Acts 2:37 NIV). In Acts, when Ananias and Sapphira lied to the Holy Spirit, Peter, speaking by the Spirit, exposed their lies, and they both dropped dead instantly (though separately).

> For the mystery of iniquity doth already work: only he who now letteth [hinders] will let [hinder], until he be taken out of the way. And then shall that Wicked be revealed, whom the Lord shall consume with the spirit of his mouth, and shall destroy with the brightness of his coming: Even him, whose coming is after the working of Satan with all power and signs and lying wonders, And with all deceivableness of unrighteousness in them that perish; because they received not the love of the truth, that they might be saved. (2 Thessalonians 2:7–10 KJV)

Accompanying our Lord are armies of saints and angels. The book of Jude quotes Enoch, the prophet, as saying, "I saw the Lord coming with tens of thousands of his saints" (Jude 1:14 KJV). We have already seen in Revelation 17:14 the promise that *his called, chosen, and faithful followers* will accompany him when he comes. This describes the church returning with the Lord when he appears in glory, and armies of angels will accompany him, multiplied millions who will return with the Lord.

4) *And he shall rule them with a rod of iron: and he treadeth the winepress of the fierceness and wrath of Almighty God. And he hath on his vesture and on his thigh a name written, KING OF KINGS, AND LORD OF LORDS. (Revelation 19:15b–16 KJV)*

This title, written on both his clothing and his thigh is linked to his judgment and his continuing rule with an iron scepter. Some Bible scholars speak of the robe as his righteousness and the thigh as a symbol of strength. When our Lord comes, he will first destroy the evil, both people and nations. Then he will rule, or *shepherd*, over the rest with a rod or staff of iron. The iron scepter is a symbol of tough justice—unbending, unwavering.

> You will rule them with an iron scepter,
> you will dash them to pieces like pottery.
> (Psalm 2:8b NIV)

Many scholars feel this is descriptive of the millennial years when righteousness will reign in all the earth. Though there will be sin and sinners present, the rule of our Christ will bring immediate justice. In John Milton's *Paradise Lost* the description of war in heaven is a drawn-out protracted battle, but Jesus said of Satan's judgment, "I beheld Satan as lightning fall from heaven" (Luke 10:18 KJV). In God's omnipotence, omniscience, and omnipresence *all things are naked and opened* before him. Judgment is immediate, even as Christians stand before Christ.

> Now if any man build upon this foundation gold, silver, precious stones, wood, hay, stubble; Every man's work shall be made manifest: for the day shall declare it, because it shall be revealed by fire; and the fire shall try every man's work of what

> sort it is. If any man's work abide which he hath built thereupon, he shall receive a reward. If any man's work shall be burned, he shall suffer loss: but he himself shall be saved; yet so as by fire. (1 Corinthians 3:12–15 KJV)

Always we should remember, "For the Father judgeth no man, but hath committed all judgment unto the Son: That all men should honour the Son, even as they honour the Father. He that honoureth not the Son honoureth not the Father which hath sent him" (John 5:22–23 KJV).

Prayer

Father, we so often have great difficulty seeing the end of all this. As the author of Genesis, you are also the author of Revelation. You are the Alpha and the Omega, you are the beginning and the end, and you are the author and the finisher of our faith. Father, bring us to yourself at just the right time. In Jesus's name. Amen.

About the Author

David M. Revell had set his sights on a career in physics with NASA, but a life-changing experience with the risen Christ in his first year of college moved him towards the ministry. In his early pulpit ministry, he also discovered the joy of the classroom and served in public and private Christian schools teaching math, science, and Bible. Doors opened for him in ministry as a pastor, teacher, Christian school principal, Bible camp teacher, and then a professor at a Christian university. He has ministered in medical and preaching missions in Russia and missions in South Africa, Nicaragua, and the Caribbean island nations.

CPSIA information can be obtained
at www.ICGtesting.com
Printed in the USA
LVHW022249220222
711709LV00009B/734